D0924387

FOR EVERY HOUSE
A GARDEN

A guide for
reproducing period gardens

Affectionately dedicated

to

mother

Giovanna Lazzaris Favretti

FOR EVERY HOUSE A GARDEN

A guide for
reproducing period gardens

by Rudy J. Favretti and
Joy P. Favretti

The
Pequot
Press

Chester, Connecticut 06412

Other books by the Favrettis

Growing for Showing — Doubleday

Colonial Gardens — Barre Press

Early New England Gardens — Sturbridge

New England Colonial Gardens — Pequot Press

Our Sacred Inheritance — Knox Foundation

Once Upon Quoketaug — Parousia Press

Highlights of Connecticut Agriculture
— Cooperative Extension Service

Copyright © 1977 by Joy and Rudy Favretti
Library of Congress Catalogue Card No. 76-051128
ISBN 0-87106-080-9
All rights reserved
First Edition
Manufactured in the United States of America

TABLE OF CONTENTS

PREFACE

Today houses from all periods are being restored and preserved. It seemed logical to create a short, authoritative book to include all eras of the past in hopes that every house will have a suitable garden.

We have kept this book brief and to the point knowing that it will be used by the gardener as he hastily prepares to do a precious weekend's worth of garden restoration or reproduction.

Mansfield, Connecticut   The Authors
1977

A GUIDE FOR STARTING
YOUR REPRODUCTION PROJECT

There is something to be said for reproducing a garden for your house that conforms to the period in which the house was built or to an era since its construction. A setting for your house that contradicts its architectural period is not as pleasing as one that conforms. A better scale relationship can easily be achieved by planting a garden in period. Also, the plants used can better accent the architecture if they are of the same style. In other words, a basic, unified landscape scheme presents a better total package than one that is composed of many discordant and conflicting styles.

The beauty of home ownership, however, is that we can do exactly as we please with our house and landscape. Therefore, if you detest the austerity of certain colonial landscapes, there is no one telling you that you must have one. Looking at a later period, certain Victorian landscapes are very costly to maintain and install and are financially prohibitive for the average American.

We intend in this booklet, however, to point out the basic characteristics of certain period landscapes, so that even if you do not wish to install a detailed landscape, you may like to use some very basic characteristics to suggest the style.

How To Start

For many it is hard to know what type of garden plan to use, where to put the garden, how to enclose it, how large it should be, whether to include vegetables and herbs as well as flowers, and how to go about installing the garden generally. It is best to hire professional assistance in the person of a landscape architect who is sympathetic towards the area of historic preservation and restoration. But, sometimes funds do not permit this type of consultation, and you may have to develop the plans yourself.

Naturally, the first thing to do is research the site, the people who lived there, and the deed or land records. Leave no stones unturned because the more you can find out the better and more individualistic the garden will be.

7

It matters not what area you research first. Let us start with the people who lived in the house. What did they do, and when did they do it? If there were several families, find data on each and determine which one or which period you will represent. An example of this type of research is that which went into the garden design for the Noah Webster House. Naturally we knew about the famous linguist, but he didn't live there after he became famous. So the obvious question was: what did his parents do? They were farmers, not wealthy, but of moderate means. The architecture of the house was simple, not elegant, further pointing to the fact that the garden should be small and simple and not contain a vast array of unusual plants such as tulips that had to be imported.

Sometimes in researching the people who live in a house, you find facts that pertain directly to gardens. The garden at the Salem Towne House at Old Sturbridge Village contains many fruit trees because Mr. Towne experimented with fruit and actually developed a new variety of apple called the "Porter". These details lend interest and individuality to a garden.

Written and published records could shed much light on the gardens of a particular site. Probate inventories often mention orchards, walls and gardens, and some have been known to have plans attached. Some probate records name fruit trees by variety. Even if the inventories or wills contain no mention of gardens, they give you an idea of the relative worth of the person. This is invaluable information because it offers guidelines concerning the size for the garden and the elegance or simplicity of the proposed plan.

Deeds can offer garden information. The authors recently came across one deed that mentions "the southwest corner of the garden west of the dwelling house" as the beginning of a boundary. Upon investigating the site, the exact dimensions of the garden were determined with relative ease.

Diaries, journals, letters and personal documents usually contain a wealth of information. One has only to read the diaries of George Washington and Thomas Jefferson to obtain quite a clear picture of gardening and agriculture. Lesser known men and women kept records, too, on such facts as when flowers came into bloom, when seeds were planted, and how and when walks were laid. Account books, while they contain only facts and figures, are invaluable because in them are such items as listings of seeds bought, crops harvested, tools purchased, and materials bought to combine with herbs for household remedies.

Personal letters, written from husband to wife, sister to sister, brother to brother, etc., reveal much because it was the custom of the day to speak of the plants in bloom in the garden, the change of season and its effect on the garden, what was harvested, and much more.

Town histories sometimes have descriptions of a garden or a site, and quite often contain sketches of houses showing their gardens and fences. John Warner Barber wrote in the early nineteenth century, "Historical Collections of Every Town . . ." for many of the states. His engravings of each town show gardens in some cases, fence styles, street tree arrangements, and many other details.

News articles and advertisements are helpful, especially in developing a list of plants. Many state and local historical societies have collections of early newspapers and broadsides. Articles sometimes appear commemorating a particular individual, and sometimes his house and grounds are mentioned. Old essays, speeches, and pamphlets are invaluable. The archives of horticultural societies are full of this type of information.

The authors rely heavily on paintings for information on the design of gardens. These works often suggest a fence style or garden arrangement typical of a particular town or region. We are aware of some murals that show village scenes that can be identified, and many of these murals illustrate gardens.

One is not often lucky enough to find a plan. How many people make a plan today? Not many. The same was true in early times and many of the plans that were made have been lost. But do not overlook this aspect of research; sometimes the files of historical societies contain them. Even if it is not the plan of the site in question, if it is in the same region or area, you might get some ideas.

While word of mouth is not considered as reliable a source as the written word, you should consider it. On asking a member of the eighth generation of the Nehemiah Williams family if there ever had been a garden in front of their old house, and if there were, had it been fenced as most of them had been, he responded in the affirmative. Upon probing the site, we found the stub of a stone fence post that had broken off, proving that there had been a fence there.

Probing the site, itself, often reveals much information. It is good to do this late in the fall when the tall grass has died down or early in the spring before it starts to grow. Then you can see the lay of the land. Sometimes you will find the remains of an old walk, and depressions on either side will suggest that there were garden beds there. Sometimes there are mounds, instead of depressions, suggesting that beds were raised. We recently discovered a cobble band around the foundation of a house. It was four to six inches below the soil surface.

Areas enclosed by walls or plants suggest that the enclosure was either a pen or a garden of some sort. One walled enclosure we found, family tradition says, was a children's play yard, which had been laid out to confine toddlers so they wouldn't stray into the woods.

An odd arrangement of trees or shrubs, having no meaning today, with careful study, might suggest a garden plan. Large shrubs and small trees around the outside of an area with a depressed or raised spot in the central portion most certainly suggest a garden.

Sometimes removing soil from these depressed or raised areas, or from around walls or house foundations will bring plants to life. Many times seeds that haven't been planted in years will germinate because they have been preserved in the depths of the soil. These may not necessarily date to the earliest period of the house, but they may suggest how a present-day garden evolved.

Should There Be A Garden?

Sometimes there were no flower gardens because only vegetable gardens were planted, and flowers and herbs needed for food, fragrance and medicine were grown among them. Maybe there were a few flowers by the front door and some herbs by the kitchen, and that is all. This is where research about the people who occupied a given house may cast light on whether or not there should be a garden, and what type it should be.

If you are thinking of a garden for your own home, there are two ways to approach the problem. If you are a purist and want things just as they were at the period of your house, proceed as suggested. But if you do not really like to garden and cannot afford to hire a gardener, then, perhaps, you should merely install the basic fabric of walks and drives and plant the essential trees and shrubs as outlined in the appropriate section of this book.

Avoid Common Faults Made In Reproducing A Garden

No reproduction, no matter how well articulated, can truly depict how a garden looked during the era it tries to represent. This is because the element of time comes into play. No matter how hard we try, our way of life greatly influences our gardens. Nevertheless, there are several common mistakes that we can avoid when reproducing a garden by observing the following:
1. For the design of your landscape, strictly follow the evidence obtained through your own research and, or, the background as set

forth in the following chapters.

2. Use plants that are authentic to the period you have decided to represent.

3. In many cases, portions of the original property have been sold off, and you are left with just a section of the original tract. Don't try to telescope the whole scheme into the small piece of ground that remains. Instead, reproduce only the part that pertains to the section you now hold. For example, if you are left with just the house and a portion of the dooryard, be content to have just a dooryard garden. Don't try to build a barn, install a vegetable garden, and crowd the landscape with fruit trees. If you do, the scale relationship will be wrong and you will lose the proper effect.

4. In the twentieth century, we have the tendency to over manicure. Decide on the period you will represent. If it is before 1860, don't mow your lawn with a rotary or reel mower. Instead, just mow it once a month with a sickle-bar type mower. This will give you a rougher surfaced lawn and one that is more in keeping with the period.

5. The fences you use should be appropriate to the landscape scheme. Enclosing a dooryard garden, or any other garden, with a split rail fence is the modern way. No garden would have been enclosed with so open a fence. Split rail fences were used to enclose fields and pastures, but gardens were enclosed with impenetrable fences, such as paling or pickets.

6. Don't fall into the herb garden trap. Specific herb gardens, as such, were rarely planted. Rather, the herbs were mixed with flowers and vegetables. A description of a garden found in *My Grandmother's Garden and an Ancestral Orchard,* by Mary Mathews Bray (1931), describes what was probably a fairly typical farmstead garden. She describes eight square beds in the center of the garden with two wide borders along the fence on the outside. The beds were divided by gravel paths and were raised by sawed boards. The author states that this garden was laid out before 1837. In regard to the arrangement of plants in the garden, she says:

> . . . in those days a garden was not usually arranged for effect as a whole . . . each plant was cherished for itself and was put where it seemed best for it individually, or often, of course, where it was most convenient.
>
> In our garden, according to the custom of the

11

PORTLAND COMMUNITY
COLLEGE LIBRARY

times, four beds were given over to herbs useful in cooking or for household remedies.

The other beds in the garden were devoted to flowers, and the borders along the outside were planted with roses and shrubs, as well as, currants.

We may discern from this description that the plan still followed the medieval prototype which will be described in the next chapter. Herbs, though grown in separate beds, were not set aside in a special garden. Other writers describe herbs mixed right into the plots with vegetables and flowers.

7. Avoid contrived features in the landscape. If no well exists on the property, building a false one is not only a waste of money but it usually looks contrived. If it is possible to restore an old well, by all means do so, but false ones rarely are effective. This concept would apply to other features as well. Gardens were not cluttered with jugs, old farm tools, ox yokes, parts of spinning wheels or other artifacts that we might now consider "quaint". This is not to say that gardens were always neat and tidy, for that is far from the case. But they were not purposely ornamented with "knick-knacks".

8. Gravel was the most common walk material used in gardens up to 1900. In the North, the next most common material was flat fieldstone, while in the South, brick was popular. In selecting fieldstone for walks, select large, stable ones. They are not only easier to walk on, but they have a better scale relationship to most gardens. Tiny flat stones are dangerous under foot and are not authentic.

Here is an old "recipe" for laying a garden walk, taken from Macjenzie's *Five Thousand Receipts in the Useful and Domestic Arts (1831):*

> The bottom should be laid with lime rubbish, large flint stones, or other hard matter, for eight to ten inches thick, to keep the weeds from growing through, and over this the gravel is to be laid six or eight inches thick. This should be laid rounding up in the middle, by which means the larger stones will run off to the sides, and may be raked away; for the gravel should never be screened before it is laid on.

> It is a common mistake to lay these walks too round, which not only makes them uneasy to walk upon, but takes off from their apparent breadth. One

inch in five feet is sufficient proportion for the rise in the middle; so that a walk of twenty feet wide should be four inches higher at the middle than at the edges, and so in proportion. As soon as the gravel is laid it should be raked, and the large stones thrown back again; then the whole should be rolled both lengthwise and crosswise; and the person who draws the roller should wear shoes with flat heels, that he may make no holes, because holes made in a new walk are not easily remedied. The walks should always be rolled three or four times after very hard showers, from which they will bind more firmly than otherwise they could ever be made to do.

9. Be cautious of foundation planting. Actually, planting a mass of shrubs along your foundation is a late Victorian and twentieth century practice. Therefore, employing this practice if you have a colonial or early nineteenth century house will not conform to a suitable landscape style. Foundation plantings were used to soften high foundations. Many late Victorian houses had foundations that were fully two, three or four feet above the soil surface. Some were even higher. If your house is low to the ground and of a period that pre-dates the 1860's or 1870's, don't plant it with an abundance of shrubs.

FARMSTEAD GARDENS
1607 - 1940

At the time of the American Revolution, about ninety-four percent of all people in this country were engaged in farming. Most of them were farming to subsist. Just a few, along the seacoast or navigable rivers, farmed commercially, but commercial farming was not then as we know it today. An average herd of cattle was about six, while today, eighty cows are common in one herd. The six percent who were not engaged in farming, such as, ministers, lawyers, innkeepers, doctors, and blacksmiths, often kept a cow, horse, pigs, and planted a large garden, because such produce was not generally available. So we might say that practically everybody was engaged in farming to some degree or other.

Historical Background

What were the gardens of our farming forefathers like? Naturally, they differed from one plot to another, but, because gardens are the outgrowth of economic and social conditions of the times, we may draw certain generalizations.

Most of the gardens of our earliest settlers at Jamestown and Plymouth were patterned after Tudor gardens, which were still very common in England. The Tudor gardens evolved from medieval gardens. In fact, most gardens throughout Europe were still based on the medieval plan, so even our earliest settlers from countries other than England laid down similar gardens.

Tudor gardens had several basic characteristics. Perhaps the first and most important was that the garden was rigidly enclosed by a high wall. Medieval gardens employed hedges or wattle fences. Enclosure was important for protection against enemies and beasts, as well as, from the weather. (fig. 1)

These ancient gardens bore little axial relationship to the house. In other words, the French concept of a strong axial vista from the main doors and windows of the palace through the extent of the gardens had yet to be conceived. Instead, the garden was situated where the exposure and soil were the best and where a convenient space remained

Figure 1. A typical medieval garden. Notice the symmetrical arrangement of garden plots, the use of fruit trees within the garden, the rail around the central portion of the garden, the well and fountain as a focus, and the strict enclosure of the whole.

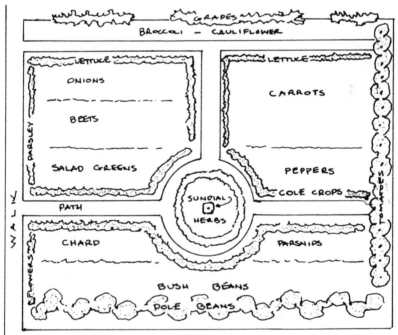

Figure 2. Plan of the authors' vegetable garden in the medieval style. A garden of this sort is easy to organize and tend and produces higher yields in a given space.

16

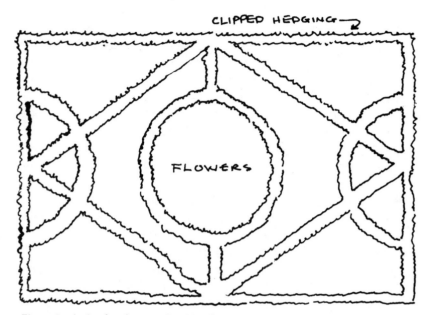

Figure 3. A plan for a knot garden. The design is created with a low, clipped hedge. The spaces between are planted with flowering plants.

between the various parts of the building and, or, buildings.

The ancient monastery garden, situated in the center of the cloistered courtyard, is a fine example of a typical medieval garden. Within its enclosure, the garden plan was highly symmetrical. It consisted of a long central path that ran from one end wall to the other. On either side of this path were garden beds or plots, then called "quarters". These beds were either square or rectangular depending on the dimensions of the garden, and each bed was devoted to the culture of a particular plant species. Plants were easy to cultivate and harvest in this manner because the gardeners had access to them from all sides, and the beds could be so divided that small quantities of certain plants had their own "quarter". In fact, this method of growing a garden makes a great deal of sense, and some gardeners today are going back to it because the yield per square foot is higher, in that the plants can be grown closer together than if planted in long rows. Mulching to reduce maintenance is easier and less costly because not as much mulch is needed. (fig. 2)

The monotony of the medieval garden plan probably gave birth to the practice of criss-crossing the quarters with paths, called "alleys", to

17

form varied geometric designs. Eventually, designs called Knots were made with plants. Knot gardens were quite popular during the Tudor period in England. (fig. 3)

Knot gardens should not be confused with French parterre gardens. They differ in that parterre designs are more sinuous and embroidered and greater restraint is shown in the use of plants. For example, in a parterre the design is made by planting low hedging material against a base of gravel or grass. Some parterres didn't use plants at all, but were merely embroidered designs in gravel against gravel. In the knot garden, on the other hand, the spaces between the knotted, hedge-like design were often filled with flowers. (fig. 4)

The beds in medieval gardens were usually raised several inches above the ground. The idea of raising beds started in Roman times as a means of adding good soil to the garden and at the same time raising the garden for convenience of maintenance and vision. Obviously, this practice persisted for years, and we find in medieval gardens highly ornamented and panelled boards used as curbs around the beds. At intervals, and especially at corners, finial topped posts accented the scheme. These fences were called "rails". (See fig. 1.)

Ornamentation, in general, was not excessive in these ancient gardens. In addition to that already mentioned, some device for bringing and holding water in the garden was included. Often it took the form of a well or cistern, placed either in the center of the main alley or at one end. Potted plants were also placed about the garden. Often these were species that were too tender for continuous culture out-of-doors. Bees and a skep to house them were also often included. During the Tudor period, a higher degree of ornamentation was employed in the form of lead statues, topiary, and carved wooden figures.

Four major groups of plants were cultivated in these ancient gardens: vegetables, herbs, flowers, and fruit. The garden plan permitted the separation of pungent herbs from vegetables, but flowers, vegetables, and other herbs were mixed. Fruit trees were often placed in the center of the quarters, and the beds along the outer enclosure of the garden were usually lined with fruit trees or arbors to support vines or espaliered fruit trees. Tables and chairs were sometimes placed under these arbors and eating out-of-doors was not uncommon.

Our Earliest Gardens

The medieval garden, with a lesser degree of rigidity and ornamentation, was what our earliest settlers knew. When they arrived upon this continent they eventually built sturdy houses out of wood, as well as, out buildings to shelter livestock and fodder, and sheds to hold

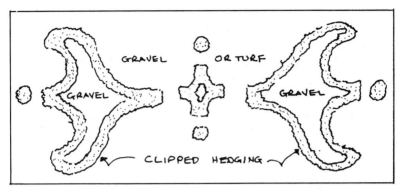

Figure 4. A plan for a parterre. The design, as with a knot, is planted with low, clipped plants. However, in this case, the spaces between are left open.

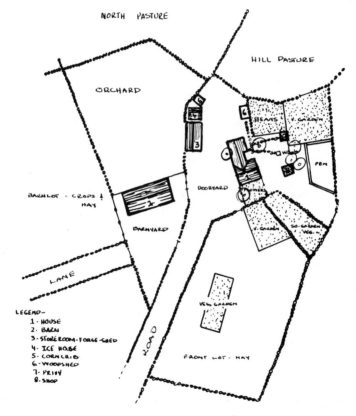

Figure 5. Plan for the Nehemiah Williams farmstead (1719). The buildings were clustered around the dooryard where much farm and household activity took place. Notice the specific gardens each placed where soil and exposure were best for the crops to be grown. The parlor garden that contained flowers and other ornamental plants was sited directly in front of the house.

19

wood for the fire and in which to perform specialized crafts. In colder climates, such as New England, the appertinent structures were sited to shield the house from the prevailing Northwest winter winds. This scheme was also useful in that the prevailing summer breezes, out of the Southwest, carried barnyard odors away.

So what evolved was a house, surrounded by farm buildings to the Northwest, with a dooryard in between. The dooryard is not to be confused with the barnyard, which was adjacent to the barn. (fig. 5) The dooryard was the center of activity. Butchering was performed here, soap was made here, wood was chopped and stacked here, clothes were washed here, and practically every outdoor activity was performed in the dooryard. This was natural because the dooryard was a circulation node and everyone had to pass through it to go to the outbuildings. Also, in the winter and early spring, it was a protected spot. Furthermore, it was the entrance to the farmstead.

Most farmers had their farmstead, which consisted of a few acres, and then somewhere else they had their meadows, fields, and woodlots. Large scale crops, such as hay, corn, and, perhaps, even pumpkins and turnips, were grown away from the homelot, but the smaller scale crops, such as, peas, cabbages, radishes, carrots, garlic, onions, leeks, melons, herbs, and beans were planted in gardens near the house. These homelot gardens were tended by the women of the household. Thomas Tusser, the sixteenth century poet, wrote:

> In March and April, from morning till night,
> In sowing and setting, good housewives delight:
> To have in a garden or otherlike plot,
> To trim up their house and to furnish the pot.

In our description of the placement of the house and outbuildings and the resulting dooryard, it is obvious that our forefathers developed a very functional plan, based on their needs and the conditions that they found. This functional concept was also carried out in the placement of their homelot gardens. As was true of medieval and Tudor gardens, farmstead gardens bore no design relationship to the house. Instead, they were situated on a southerly slope to trap the early spring sunlight so that peas, onions, lettuce and radishes could be planted early. Good soil was another important factor in selecting the garden site.

We find, then, that gardens were laid down wherever conditions were best, without any design consideration whatsoever. The garden

Figure 6. Picket fences have been built for centuries in endless variation. On the left is shown the earliest type, merely a pointed sapling set into the ground.

might have been to the East, South or West of the house or ten, twenty or one hundred feet away. It might have been parallel to the house or at an odd or curious angle, expressing the lay of the land and exposure, rather than a relationship to the whole. Sometimes, if the housewife was a lover of flowers, a little, enclosed garden near the door of the house was filled with plants as she acquired them, adding a touch of color and pleasure to all who passed by.

The plan of these early gardens followed that of the Tudor gardens described above, but without very much ornamentation. They were enclosed by palings and pickets as these were the best kinds of fences for excluding livestock and wild animals. Later, where stone was plentiful, fieldstone walls were built which gave better protection against the winds and, in addition, trapped the heat of the sun. (fig. 6)

The system of planting in plots, beds or blocks continued, but not always in the rigidly symmetrical scheme of medieval and Tudor gardens. In fact, often there was no symmetrical arrangement at all but rather just a series of trodden earth paths between plots of like plants of varying size.

The concept of raising beds prevailed, but not in such an ornamented fashion. The idea of raising beds was useful as a means of improving drainage. Oftentimes, beds were raised simply by mounding without providing any kind of curbing whatsoever. Other times rough saplings cut from the forest were pegged in place to hold the soil. Until water-powered sawmills became common, sawn boards were rarely used as curbs for raised beds.

Because there was not a shortage of land, fruit trees were banished early from farmstead gardens in this country. Instead, they were planted about the dooryard and certain tender species, such as peaches and apricots, were planted on the southerly side of building and walls so they could benefit from wind protection and trapped heat. Apples and pears, the mainstays, were set out in the dooryard in places where they would not interfere with the many activities or shade the little dooryard garden.

Vine and shrub fruits, on the other hand, were retained in the enclosed gardens as were strawberries. As gardening evolved, the plan sometimes included a special fruit garden. Grapes were grown on crude trellises, often against a shed or wall. Elaborate arbors were rarely constructed.

There are few accounts of knot gardens in America. This is probably because these gardens took considerable labor in planting and care, and as our early settlers had to devote most of their time to "carving out the land" to suit their needs, there was little time left for the art of gardening.

Bees, on the other hand, were often a feature of our early gardens. Their value as pollinators and honey producers was much appreciated. Hence, bees were incorporated into the garden and orchard. An elaborate skep was not always present because a hollowed log would serve as well.

Eighteenth Century Farm Gardens

The gardens just described were not only associated with the first century of our colonial period, but the same general plan prevailed into the eighteenth century. We have studied many farms of eighteenth century America, and the plan shown here from the Nehemiah Williams farm in Stonington, Connecticut, is characteristic. (See fig. 5.)

In this plan, notice how the buildings surround the dooryard and form an enclosed space. The gardens (stippled) are situated at very odd angles to the house, and their only relationship to the house is their close proximity. The south garden is probably the oldest garden on the place, judging from its favorable southerly exposure and its broken down soil structure which indicates that it has been gardened for many, many years. As was the practice through the years, specific gardens were laid down for particular crops. The south garden was always the spot for early spring vegetables. The vegetable garden adjacent to it was primarily for asparagus and small fruits, such as, strawberries, raspberries, currants and gooseberries.

Nearer the house and protected by a very high wall to the North is the bean garden. Here were set pole after pole of many varieties of beans for baking. The garden next to the bean garden was planted with potatoes.

In the middle of the front lot is another garden. Here the soil was moist and mellow, though late to thaw in the spring. However, conditions were ideal for late plants, such as: corn, cabbages, squash, pumpkins, later beans, and during the nineteenth century, tomatoes and peppers. Second planting of the early spring crops, such as, beets and carrots, were also sowed here.

Immediately in front of the house on the south side is a fenced in dooryard or parlor garden. It is not known whether or not this garden existed during the early part of the eighteenth century, though hearsay implies that it did. But certainly it was a thriving garden during the later part of that century and into the nineteenth century as well. Here the women of the house planted roses, perennials, and possibly herbs, as well as, fragrant annuals. The entire space within these parlor gardens was not necessarily devoted to flowers. A variety of plans prevailed depending upon the interest of the housewife and the time she had to devote to her garden. (fig. 7)

Fruit trees were planted about the dooryard. Two or three peach trees stood south of the woodshed along the wall. Apple and pear trees filled the area between the shop and the pen to the east. There were three pear trees along the wall that separated the parlor garden and the vegetable garden. Grape vines grew against the shop and the storeroom (granary). And, of course, a large, fifty tree orchard was planted west of the storeroom.

The entire dooryard area, not already taken up by buildings and gardens, was grass. Rock outcroppings were visible within the grass, and no attempt was ever made to remove them. The grass was mowed three or four times a year with a broad-bladed scythe. In the late nineteenth century, with the advent of the lawn mower, weekly mowings were instituted.

There was no clear or crisp definition between the graveled road which approached the Williams farm and the grass area. Instead, the gravel vignetted into the grass. Where major activities, such as, wood sawing and chopping, took place in the dooryard, large, bare spots

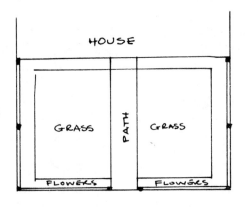

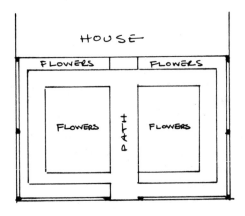

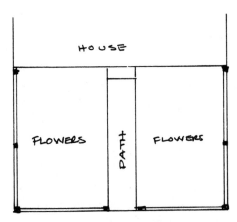

Figure 7. Arrangements for parlor gardens varied with the owner. Here are three typical plans.

appeared. In other words, a manicured lawn was not evident.

Chickens, guinea fowl and ducks scratched in the barnyard and occasionally strayed to the dooryard. In the evening, the apple trees near the shop served as a roosting place for guinea hens.

Stepping stone walks traversed the lawn in direct lines to the woodshed, privy and the well. In the fork of the walks leading to the privy and well was a large, flat stone on which tubs were placed for laundering. The adjoining grass area served as a drying yard. Immediately we see where a portion of the dooryard may have been relegated to particular farm chores: butchering, wood chopping, etc., while the other portion of the dooryard was set aside for household chores. We would imagine that such an arrangement would vary with the property in question, although we have observed that many farms had this type of division.

A few shade trees were included in the scheme. One stood in the parlor garden to the front of the house, at its westernmost end. Another stood by the kitchen door in the ell portion of the house. Another shaded the "laundering rock". Aside from a large clump of lilacs in the southeast corner of the parlor garden, few shrubs studded the landscape.

Nineteenth and Twentieth Century Farm Gardens

The plan just described prevailed throughout the nineteenth and twentieth centuries, except during the nineteenth century, more ornamental plants were added to the parlor garden, and vines, such as, wisterias, honeysuckles, and climbing roses were planted on trellises against the house and upon little arbors arching doorways. Ornamental shade trees, such as, catalpas and locusts, found their way into the dooryard, but this practice never became excessive because much of the space within the dooryard had to remain open in order to perform the many chores.

Ornamental shrubs were added to the parlor garden. Spirea and forsythia adorned its edges, and some of these shrubs were planted at the corner of buildings outside of the parlor garden as well. But again, this practice never rigidly took hold because straying livestock often chewed the shrubs to the ground, so it was better to plant them in enclosed areas.

One nineteenth century practice was to plant trees to commemorate births in the family or special patriotic events. These were often planted to outline or shade the approach road to the farmstead, or as a shadetree near the house. (fig. 8)

In the twentieth century, up to World War II, little change

25

Figure 8. The large maples surrounding this house were planted to commemorate births of family members and special events.

occured in farm gardens; but after the war, many changes took place. Wall and fence enclosures were replaced to accommodate expanded operations. Because of rapid expansion in the size of farm flocks and herds and the highly mechanized manner in which farming was conducted, small enclosed gardens were, in most cases, abandoned in favor of larger plots that could be tilled by a tractor. Consequently, the small beds where plants were grown broadcast gave way to long rows spaced far enough apart to accommodate tractor tillage.

GARDENS OF CITY MERCHANTS AND COUNTRY GENTLEMEN 1620 - 1860

The gardens of city merchants and country gentlemen before the American Revolution were very much the same layout as those of farmers. In other words, both were influenced by their medieval prototype. However, in the case of merchants and gentry, the gardens were sometimes more elaborate.

After the Revolution, we begin to see a gradual disappearance of symmetry, especially in the country estates, with a high degree of informality appearing. That is to say, the rigid symmetry of the medieval type garden gives way to curved paths and the informal placement of trees and shrubs.

Historical Background

The medieval type gardens already described in the last chapter were the basis for garden design throughout the Tudor period in England (1485 - 1603) and, also, during the reign of the Stuarts (1603 - 1714). By the time of William and Mary (1689 - 1702), these rigidly symmetrical gardens had become highly ornamented with topiary and geometric parterre hedging. The central walkway in these gardens was the major vista, and this axis was usually oriented very strongly with the main garden entrance from the palace or mansion. This was obviously a French influence, since one of the major characteristics of a French Renaissance garden is the magnificent central axis-vista.

In Stuart England, this central axis walk or vista was usually much less extensive and magnificent than in France and was often broken by a circular bed or pond (pool) in the center. The extent of the axial vista, and in turn the garden, depended a great deal upon the amount of land available, as well as, on the wealth of the owner. (fig. 9)

Parterres and knots were worked into the garden scheme as were mazes and labyrinths. Labyrinths were used extensively as a source of amusement and pleasure.

This type of garden prevailed in England from ancient times until the late eighteenth century. In summation, there were several characteristics that formed the basic design of the garden:

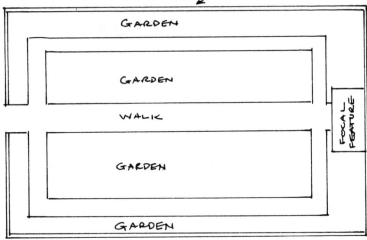

Figure 9. Typical central axis garden plan.

1. There was a long central axis walk in the center of the garden which linked the garden to the house and formed a vista through the extent of the garden.

2. This axis walk was often broken in the center or at intervals with pools of water or circular or square beds. These beds sometimes contained an exotic piece of topiary or sculpture.

3. The vista-walkway often terminated with a feature, such as, a mount, a gate, or some other ornamental point of interest.

4. On either side of this central axis were beds that mirrored each other. In other words, they were identical in size and often in plant material. Sometimes, however, the plant material and the arrangement of parterre hedging was not identical on either side of the central axis.

5. Secondary walks were laid down perpendicular to the central axis, and these too may have terminated with an ornamental feature. (See figure 9.)

6. These gardens were enclosed by a rigid wall or hedge, usually a wall, and along this wall were beds for shrubs, fruit trees, and flowers.

7. Ornamentation, usually in the form of topiary, adorned the garden. In Tudor times, lead and wooden sculpture was common, but, by

28

the reign of William and Mary, topiary was the rage.

8. Plants grown in these gardens were largely ornamental. By this time, vegetables were planted in their own separate walled garden.

The following quotations from *A New System of Agriculture* by John Lawrence (London, 1776) describes these ancient gardens:

> Place the flower garden near the house . . . because such Beauty and Ornament, the more they are under constant Inspection, the easier and better they entertain those two finer Senses, Seeing and Smelling . . .

Lawrence further states that the form of the garden

> . . . will vary to persons different Fancies; yet ought to throw the whole into Variety amidst Uniformity . . . care must be taken to contrive it so that it may be easily seen, that the curious Artist may find Admittance to the beds in every Part, either by large or lesser Gravel Walks or Paths; so as by the Reach of the Arm every Operation may be performed with Ease . . . and I think I need just say, the Center in the Middle of the Circle should be filled with some curious Ever-Green Plant cut pyramidically or in a spiral line . . .

Obviously, Lawrence is describing a smaller garden than the ones at Hampton Court or other such palaces; the general design scheme was the same but on a smaller scale.

In the early eighteenth century, the English, or at least their leaders, were not only disenchanted by the reign of the Stuarts but were equally disenchanted by their gardens as well. Alexander Pope (1688 - 1744) expressed not only his own sentiment about them but that of other writers and poets when he wrote the following excerpted from the *Guardian*:

> ADAM and *Eve* in Yew; *Adam* a little shatter'd by the fall of the Tree of Knowledge in the great Storm; *Eve* and the Serpent very flourishing.
>
> THE Tower of *Babel*, not yet finished.
>
> St. GEORGE in Box; his Arm scarce long enough, but will be in a Condition to stick the Dragon by next *April*.
>
> A *green Dragon* of the same, with a Tail of Ground-Ivy for the present.
>
> N.B. *These two not to be Sold separately.*

EDWARD the *Black Prince* in Cypress.

A *Laurustine* Bear in Blossom, with a Juniper Hunter in Berries.

A Pair of Giants, *stunted*, to be sold cheap.

A Queen *Elizabeth* in Phylyraea, a little inclining to the Green Sickness, but of full growth.

ANOTHER Queen *Elizabeth* in Myrtle, which was very forward, but Miscarried by being too near a Savine.

AN old Maid of Honour in Wormwood.

A topping *Ben Johnson* in Lawrel.

DIVERS eminent Modern Poets in Bays, somewhat blighted, to be disposed of a Pennyworth.

A Quick-set Hog shot up into a Porcupine, by its being forgot a Week in rainy Weather.

A Lavender Pig with Sage growing in his Belly.

NOAH's *Ark* in Holly, standing on the Mount; the Ribs a little damaged for want of Water.

A Pair of *Maidenheads* in Firr, in great forwardness.

The geometric parterres and bold topiary was considered a strong influence of William of Orange (William III) and, therefore, thought to be very Dutch, rigid, and unnatural. Pope and his fellow literati, as well as, the wealthy landed gentry favored a more natural type of garden. They chose to banish straight lines, as well as, flower beds from the landscape in favor of serpentine walks, plantings of tree groups in large expanses of lawn and large informal lakes. The string and the stake were abandoned as tools for garden layout.

These new gardens were vast parks often taking up hundreds of acres. They were meant to walk in, and most of them had a road system that meandered along the boundary of the park from which one could get glimpses of the landscape within the garden, as well as, without. Because the road girded the garden it was called a "belt road".

Temples, both ruined, classic and gothic, were included in these gardens and were intended to be not just garden ornaments, but to have artistic and political significance as well. Inspiration for their placement was derived from paintings by famous artists of Italian landscapes of a century earlier. Paintings by Lorrain and Poussin, as well as, the more picturesque scenes by Rosa were collected by the owners of these gardens and were used as the basis for the design. (fig. 10)

Figure 10. The Temple of Ancient Virtue at Stowe, Buckinghamshire, England.

Busts of Greek philosophers were placed in the temples to inspire political, as well as, philosophical thinking and reaction. As the garden owners and their guests strolled along the serpentine paths, they stopped at the temples and discussed the political problems of the day. Some temples were even built as ruins to display reaction to certain political doctrine; the ruined temple symbolized the doctrine's projected downfall.

The "English landscape garden" (as these gardens were called) was natural in intent as opposed to the rigid formality of gardens of a previous era. One might argue that including temples in gardens was not natural. But two hundred seventy years ago, even artists who painted landscapes felt that a landscape could not stand by itself as a painting, and for this reason, Claude Lorrain, as an example, included temples in his landscapes.

The countryside became part of the garden landscape by use of the foss or ha-ha wall. These vast landscaped gardens were surrounded by a ha-ha in order that one might look across the landscape and see deer or cattle grazing, but yet these creatures could not surmount the ha-ha to enter the garden. Also, it appeared from the center of the garden that

Figure 11. A typical ha-ha wall, cut into the natural slope so as not to visually disturb the flow of the natural contours from a distance.

there was no fence or enclosure present because the wall was sunken and the natural grade of the terrain was apparently not broken. (fig. 11) From within the garden there were extensive vistas through the large groupings of trees to the surrounding landscape.

Four names are associated with this type of garden which was first built in England and later spread to France ("jardin anglais") and the rest of Europe. Sir John Vanbrugh built himself a garden of this sort at Claremont in Surrey, and he later advised on others of this type. Charles Bridgeman, who had been gardener to Queen Anne, was called to revise the original formal gardens at Stowe. It was he who introduced the ha-ha wall there. William Kent carried on at Stowe after the death of Bridgeman and developed the design in the natural style that is visible there today. And while Kent was working at Stowe, Lancelot Brown was the head gardener. Soon Lancelot Brown became a designer of landscapes in the natural style and is known to have landscaped about two hundred gardens.

Brown, known as "Capability Brown," was considered the master of the natural style after the death of William Kent in 1748. He further banished flowers from the garden and, in addition, landscaped large estates with utmost simplicity. In fact, unless forced by the owner to include them, he eventually banished temples and walled gardens from his landscapes, and his layouts became an undulating blend of masses of trees, bodies of water, and acres of grass. His landscaped "parks" began at the outer four walls of the house and, within vision of the house, he usually sited a large serpentine lake. The surrounding belt of trees was planted informally, some trees in clumps and others singly to obtain a "natural effect."

Brownian landscapes were only effective if the garden were several hundred acres in size. Most of his lakes were at least five acres. Brown emphasized the play of light, shade and perspective in his landscapes.

After Brown's death in 1783, Sir Humphrey Repton emerged as his successor to landscaping in the natural style. By this time, however, large land tracts for creating landscaped "parks" were fewer, and Repton was forced to deal with smaller parcels. Brown, in his designs, had dealt with only a few species of trees (oaks, chestnuts, beeches, lindens) to achieve supreme simplicity. Repton, on the other hand, used a varied list of species. He also reintroduced the flower garden to the landscape. It was sited near the house, where it had been in past eras, and provided an immediate foreground to the view from the house. He retained the natural landscape style in the background.

Repton bore the brunt of a great deal of criticism from a group of individuals who favored the "picturesque style" in landscaping. They said that what Repton, and Brown before him, planned and planted was not natural at all. Instead they recommended creating a landscape studded with a series of paintable scenes that would include thickets, vines growing up trees, rustic fences, and a combination of evergreens with deciduous trees.

Still later, a landscape style called "gardenesque" by the man who proposed it, J. C. Loudon (1783 - 1843), advanced that trees, shrubs, and flowers were the most important part of the landscape, and everything else in it should be secondary. Features such as Capability Brown's play of undulating lines of the water's edge with the green turf before a background of trees, and the play of light and shadow among the tree masses, became secondary. With the gardenesque style emerges the Victorian mode of landscaping.

Gardens of Merchants and Country Gentlemen in the American Colonies

The gardens adjacent to the houses of merchants in town, as well as, those in the country were quite like the Stuart gardens described in the brief historical background. They contained several characteristics that

Figure 12. This painting entitled "Mansion House with Figures" shows a typical, symmetrical garden plan with the central walkway.

were common in most American gardens from the early seventeenth century to about the time of the Revolutionary War. These characteristics were as follows:

Major central walkway - A long axis walk was the main feature of the garden. It was as long as the owner could afford to have it and was paved in gravel, brick, or stone, depending upon the climate and the availability of materials. These walks were anywhere from four to fifteen feet in width and in scale with the overall size of the garden. Other walks connected with the main one at right angles if the garden were large enough to warrant such an extensive system. (fig. 12)

Beds for flowers - On either side of the main walk, beds for flowers and herbs mirrored each other. There were narrow walks between these flower beds because, as you will recall from the quote by Laurence previously mentioned, it was important to be able to reach the beds for ease in cultivation.

Terminal features - At the end of the main axis walk or the major secondary walks, terminal features or focal points would often be sited. Such features might have consisted of a summer house, an arbor, a sundial or armillary sphere, topiary, a tool or seed house, a well or cistern, or any

34

Figure 13. Two examples of summerhouses. The one on the left is characteristic of the 18th century while the one on the right represents a popular late 19th century style.

other features useful to conducting everyday activities in the garden or for enjoying the garden scenery. Summer houses, either completely enclosed or opensided, seemed to be the most popular feature, while arbors were the second most popular. They were sometimes placed on a mount or rise of ground to gain a better prospect. Topiary and sundials were more popular as a central focus in the center of the main axis walk. (fig. 13)

Trees in the garden - In beds along the outer fence or wall, fruit trees of various sorts were often grown. Because they cast shade upon the garden, they were usually underplanted with such shade tollerant plants as: lilies-of-the-valley, violets, primroses, and spring flowering bulbs. Not every garden contained fruit trees, especially if it were small. But because fruit growing was popular, trees were included if space permitted, especially pears and peaches, because they grew more upright and shaded a smaller area.

Enclosures - This type of garden was enclosed by either a fence, hedge, or wall. Walls of brick or stone were most popular in the city, while fences seemed most common in villages and in the country. Fence height in a community was often determined by town law. Fences in front, along the street, were usually specified to be shorter than those

35

along the side and rear.

It was not uncommon to make side fences of solid board, five or six feet in height. Pickets, in great variety, seemed to be the most popular type for front fences. Pickets were extremely useful in excluding animals and wildlife because they were virtually impenetrable, and at the same time most types permitted the free flow of air into the garden. When solid board fences were used the upper two feet was sometimes louvered for air circulation. Hedges were not as tight as board or picket fences, but in come cases they were used, especially when the garden was quite large and therefore costly to enclose by a wall or fence. This was certainly the case in this century when the cost for constructing a fence became prohibitive. However, even in earlier times, gardens were hedged rather than fenced for yet another reason. If the garden were large and enclosed by a high wall, winter wind might create air currents which would be detrimental to the overwintering of plants within. By using hedges, the wind's force could be broken as it blew through. John Lawrence commented on this point,

> Walls are some defence, where they are tall and the Garden little; but otherwise they occasion great Reverberations, Whirles, and Currents of wind, so they often do more harm than good. I should therefore choose to have the Flower-garden encompassed with Hedges . . .

The type of garden which we have just described prevailed in America on city lots until the present century. Because the lots were relatively small, a rigid rectalinear plan was most efficient in that it repeated the rectangular shape of the lot. It would have been very difficult to install a plan in the natural style because there would not have been room enough to achieve the desired effects created by informal groups of trees naturally growing on a vast rolling lawn.

American gardens of this style were not as extensive as their predecessors in Europe, and they were generally simpler in appearance in that not as much ornamentation was employed. The fences of wood (because it was plentiful) did not give the same effect as the high brick walls with their refined coping. Topiary was much less popular in America. Pools of water in the center of the central axis walk never gained great popularity here.

In the nineteenth century, walk patterns in enclosed gardens were sometimes curved to make them fit better between the round beds that were coming into vogue. But the basic scheme remained the same

36

Figure 14. In this painting entitled "View of the Seat of Colonel Boyd, Portsmouth, New Hampshire" you can see the central walkway aligned with the main door of the house. Also there are secondary walks leading to various parts of the garden.

excepting that the central axis walk blended with paved or gravel paths between the round beds on either side.

The enclosed garden was popular even on country estates. The garden was usually at the rear of the country house or at its side, and the central walkway was an extension of the central hallway of the house. If no central hallway existed, the garden walk was oriented with one of the main doorways. In some cases, however, these gardens were placed across the road which passed by the house so that house and garden were physically, but not visually, separated. This was often necessitated by factors such as topography and exposure. (fig. 14)

There are many descriptions of these enclosed gardens. The gardens of Governor Winthrop in Boston in the 1600's followed this general pattern. In the next century, John Hancock's garden on Beacon Hill was based on this scheme. The beds in his garden were outlined with boxwood. The Pratt gardens near Philadelphia were also based on this ancient concept. Most of the gardens restored at Williamsburg were designed in this style, complete with hedge, parterre and topiary. (fig. 15)

By the late eighteenth century, owners of country estates had read, visited or heard about the English landscape garden. George Washington modified the approach to Mount Vernon with a pear-shaped drive enclosed by a belt of mixed ornamental trees. He also

37

Figure 15. A typical Williamsburg garden complete with hedges, parterres and topiary.

planted an informal grove of trees near the mansion and installed a ha-ha wall so that he, too, could have an integration of the surrounding countryside with his lawn. (fig. 16)

Later, Thomas Jefferson planned his grounds with a round-about walkway, ornamented with flower beds. He, too, planted trees informally near his house and in a grove nearby. Jefferson, like Washington, had read extensively about the English naturalistic style and had made extensive notes while touring English gardens in the mid 1780's.

Bernard McMahon (c. 1775 - 1816), a seedsman in Philadelphia, wrote *The American Gardener's Calendar* in 1806. It contained monthly

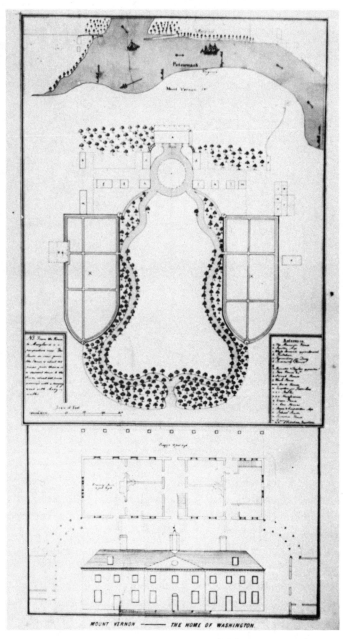

Figure 16. This plan of Mount Vernon shows the pear shaped approach to the mansion lined with plantings of ornamental trees. Notice that the flower garden (left) and kitchen garden (right) are in the ancient style.

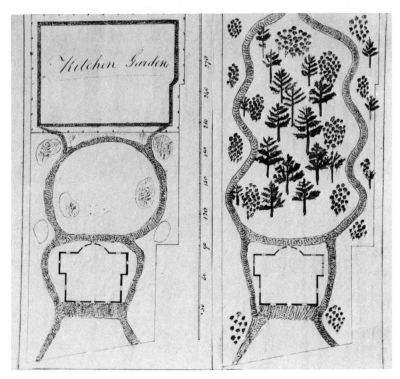

Figure 17. The gardens proposed for the Elias Hasket Derby house are typical of those advocated by McMahon. Notice the meandering walkways and the informal groupings of trees surrounding them.

tips for gardening and, also, comments on laying out grounds in the new style. He stated that formal walks were "almost abolished." McMahon emphasized that straight walks with regular intersections, square grass plots, corresponding parterres, quadrangular and angular spaces and ". . . other uniformities as in ancient design . . ." were becoming a thing of the past.

According to McMahon, when laying out grounds, one should consult nature. Varied forms and dimensions should be used, and winding walks, all bounded with plantations of trees, shrubs and flowers in various clumps, must be included.

He further advised that the house should be sited on a rise of ground with the pleasure grounds contiguous to it. An open lawn, widening from the house outward, was to be encircled by a roundabout walkway which should be bounded by trees, shrubs and flowers in clumps and thickets.* He suggested that the walks of gravel in front of the house might be 15 - 20 feet wide, obviously, to accommodate a carriage, and that the walks that entered the tree and shrub planting be narrower. These walks were to wind and meander, sometimes even turn abruptly, and often branch. (fig. 17)

McMahon also recommended the use of the ha-ha "to extend the prospect of the adjacent fields . . ." He recommended placing them at the end of the pleasure grounds. He also believed that water should be used wherever possible in the form of pools, brooks or cascades. Other forms of ornamentation, such as, statues in the lawn, were acceptable.

McMahon's book went through several printings and obviously had some effect on the laying out of country estates. However, in 1849, another man wrote a book that had a very strong and generalized influence on architectural and landscape design. His name was Andrew Jackson Downing (1815 -1852) and his book was entitled *A Treatise on the Theory and Practice of Landscape Gardening.* This work, as well as others he wrote, was extremely well written, logically organized, and easy to read. The times were ripe, we were a new nation, technology was advancing, and people seemed to be ready for a new style of architecture and landscape design. This new book, therefore, was very well received by the public and had numerous printings.

Downing's ideas were greatly influenced by the natural style of England and especially by Repton and Loudon. He greatly admired Loudon and edited a garden book by Mrs. Loudon for American audiences. Downing favored the landscape that followed the natural dictates of the site and expressed the needs of the owner. The meandering, branching walks, which were recommended, blended well with undulating land forms for a unified and compatible landscape. He also agreed that flowers and ornamental shrubs and trees should be used in the landscape, and that the garden should be a place to display these plants in a tasteful manner.

Downing disliked the ancient style for laying out a garden, though he admitted that where the space was small, such as in town or city, it was no doubt the best plan. Though he did not like Greek Revival architecture, he did feel that ancient garden designs conformed with it. He also agreed that when a garden was so close to a house as to become a part of it, the ancient style might fit better with its rectangular form.

Andrew Jackson Downing preferred Tudor, Italianate, and

*The word thicket as used in this text does does not mean an entangled mass of plants and vines but rather a mixed grouping of trees and shrubs.

Figure 18. Examples of Tudor (top), Italianate (center) and Gothic (bottom) architecture advocated by Downing because it complimented the landscape better.

Gothic architecture because he felt that the turrets, towers, peaks and irregular form of the building and roofline blended better with the natural style. In his books, as well as in his articles in *The Horticulturist*, which he edited, he presented many house plans which he and his colleague Andrew Jackson Davis had drawn. Included were comments on how to lay out the grounds for these houses. (fig. 18)

Downing advanced many basic design principles for laying out properties which ranged in size from a one acre lot to large estates, composed of 100 acres or more. Underlying all his designs was the objective of a perfect interplay of the grass covered ground with trees and water. Downing advocated selecting a natural site that contained these elements, as well as a rolling topography. He was very much at home in his native Hudson River valley for there the topography and natural scenery offered the perfect basis for a garden.

In his books, Downing brought out the point that it is important to have all parts of the landscape suited to one another. The architecture should conform to the landscape and vice-versa. This is why he planted pointed trees to compliment the peaks and turrets of his architecture. Or we could say that he selected the architecture to conform to the pointed trees.

His plans consisted of a landscape made up of several distinct spaces. These were: the approach to the house, the lawn area immediately surrounding the house, the service area, a wooded walk, an orchard, a vegetable garden, and the barn area. He felt strongly that these spaces should be distinctly separated, one from the other, with thickets of shrubs. This separation of functions is a concept that is still followed very much today.

The House and Its Approach

Like McMahon, Downing proposed that the house, whether a small Gothic cottage or a large, sprawling Italianate Villa, be sited on a rise of ground so that it would command a good prospect of the surrounding countryside, and, also, so that it would be prominent within the landscape as the major feature. He also advocated that the house be set back from the street enough so that it could have a good approach, consisting of a curved gravel drive. On small properties, the graveled drive might have consisted of a circular arc with an entrance and exit onto the street, or it might have been a single driveway with an internal turn-around, complete with a center island, probably containing a large evergreen tree. For his larger properties, he suggested setting the house far back, so that, from the slowly curving drive, fine

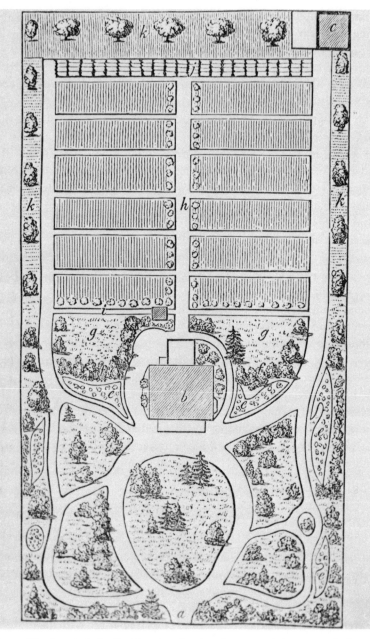

Figure 19. A typical plan by Downing showing the approach, lawn near the house, walkways, informal tree groups, and flower beds.

vistas to the house could be made through the trees. While he was a proponent of a slowly curving drive, which was intended to create the illusion of an extensive property, he warned against making the driveway so tortuous as to be ineffecient. (fig. 19) As the driveway approached the house it widened to 15 - 20 feet or more; these large forecourts were necessary to that carriages could easily turn around and, also, to accomodate several standing carriages.

Downing did not propose a specific plan for all situations. He advised his readers to study the site and let it dictate the approach scheme, as well as, the house site.

The House Setting

Downing recommended that the house be surrounded by lawn. Even though these were days before the lawnmower, lawns were mowed several times during the season with a broad-bladed scythe. Where flower beds and vulnerable shrubs were not a problem, sheep were grazed to keep the grass short; however, they would not have been grazed in the immediate house area.

Many of Downing's plans showed a drying yard, near the rear or service door of the dwelling, where clothes might be laid out to dry or hung on a line. In many of his plans, he recommended a large lawn area to the rear of the house, surrounded by a belt or thicket of shrubs. This concept is exactly like the one forwarded by McMahon. Downings favorite shrubs for thickets or "belts" were: Mockorange (Philadelphus), Lilac (Syringa), Arborvitae (Thuja), Mezereum (Daphne), Cornellian Cherry (Cornus mas), Flowering Quince (Chaenomeles), Hawthorn (Crataegus), and Spindle Tree (Euonymus). (fig. 20)

Although Downing did feel that the natural landscape formed the basis for the man-made garden, he did recommend embellishing the site with certain ornaments. Like Repton and Loudon, he advocated that flowers be returned to the landscape, especially near walks (as Thomas Jefferson had done) though he preferred the circular beds near the house. (fig. 21) Apparently he felt that flowers should be near the house where people could see them and smell them at close range. In fact, he recommended planting fragrant flowers near windows so that the fragrance could drift into the house on a summer breeze.

Downing favored flower beds surrounded by turf rather than by gravel walks. He noted that in the summer, when there is a lack of rainfall, beds in gravel look dryer than those in turf. Several of his books and articles offer plans for involved parterre designs laid in a turf background. For lawn flower beds Downing suggested low annual flowers in masses, even only one variety to the bed, sometimes with an

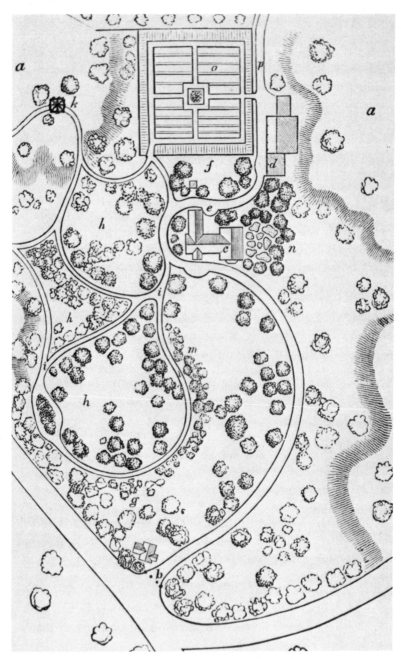

Figure 20. In the lower left, thickets of trees and shrubs may be seen. They were used to separate spaces in the landscape.

Figure 21. Flower beds in circular or oblong shapes were sited near the house so that they might be seen while approaching the house as well as through the windows when looking out.

edging of another sort. He stressed using annuals that bloomed over a long season as opposed to species like candytuft, for example, that had a short blooming period.

For beds at the edge of the lawn, such as those that might be used along a boundary fence, Downing suggested gardens with a curving or undulating edge which he called an "arabesque." His idea was that a gently undulating border, through the dips in its outline, gave an illusion of greater space. He especially recommended these for small peoperties. Here he suggested "mingled flowers," meaning a mixture of species. (fig. 22)

Downing tended to agree with Loudon that planting flowers in vases (urns) was "reducing a work of art to a mere flower pot." They believed that the urns should be used only near a house or building because they were too architectural to use in the natural landscape.

The foundation planting, which became very popular in the late nineteenth century, was not used or recommended during Downing's

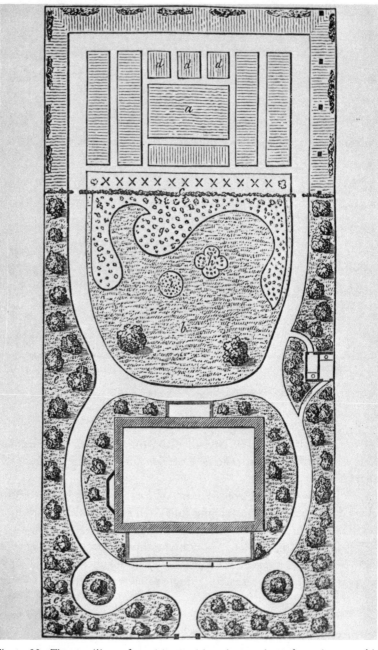

Figure 22. The curvilinear form (g) separating the rear lawn from the vegetable garden is an arabesque flower garden.

48

Figure 23. An example of tree grouping as recommended by Downing. Notice that trees within a group are unevenly spaced and that certain trees are spaced singly.

time. Downing believed that shrubs should be planted in belts or thickets and that only occasional ones should be planted near the house for interest and fragrance.

Trees

Downing was a great advocate of trees in the landscape. First of all, he suggested that good, natural groves of trees be left, and that walkways of gravel be layed out through them. He wanted the walks to meander in curving lines through the trees so that a feeling of expansiveness would prevail. Where the walks came close to one another, a thicket of shrubs was to be planted to separate and screen them. In this manner, a person walking along the path could not see that he had been close to that route before. (fig. 23)

Like Brown, Downing urged the planting of informal groups of trees in the lawn, but unlike him, he proposed a variety of species in mixed groups. He especially liked the picturesque effect created by the abrupt, jagged outline of evergreens mingled with deciduous trees. He referred to Larches, Balsam Fir, White Pine, Hemlock, and Norway Spruce as "spirited trees" because of their pointed form. (fig. 24)

Downing also recommended that some trees be planted singly so that they would grow into full, rounded, individual specimens and achieve a "beautiful effect." Popular species for this treatment were Osage Orange, Umbrella Magnolia (M. tripetala), and Maple.

Both in the design of his tree plantings and his shrub plantings, Downing was careful to achieve a unified whole, even while using a variety of plant material. He recommended doing this by repeating many of the key plants in the layout to give skeletal structure, and then by varying the secondary plants. Downing also felt that harmony could be achieved by planning coordinated color with flowers and autumn coloration.

49

Figure 24. Pointed trees were considered picturesque and repeated architectural elements of the house.

Walkways

Walkways were important in these plans because they permitted the owner and his guests to get exercise and pleasure as they strolled through the garden. Also, by meandering throughout, the walks gave the illusion of space. (See fig. 19.)

At studied intervals along the way, benches were installed. Rustic benches, conforming to the natural setting, were recommended. Some of these were covered and sited in a secluded spot for proper repose. Others were set under a picturesque tree or landscaped with a thicket of shrubs. (fig. 25)

At an appropriate point, usually on a rise of ground and commanding a view of the surrounding terrain, a rustic summerhouse was built. The summerhouse was often at the furthest spot in the garden or, at least, after the stroller had walked quite a distance. Both these rustic summerhouses and covered seats were vine-covered to render them more picturesque.

To further the cause of the picturesque along the way, waterfalls were sometimes built in streams, and vines were planted on trees.

50

Figure 25. A rustic bench and covered seat or summerhouse as one might find along a meandering walkway.

Downing liked rocks in his landscape, but suggested that if ledges were too harsh and jagged that vines be planted over them.

A portion of the property was usually set aside for an orchard and also for a vegetable garden. These sites were chosen on the basis of soil and exposure and the ornamental landscape was worked in around them. Downing did not consider the vegetable garden to be a thing of beauty, and most of his plans show it screened by a shrub border or a vine-covered trellis. His plans for the vegetable garden were quite like the ancient scheme, with fruit trees espaliered on the boundary fence or grown as standard trees, the vegetable plots being along the walks in the center.

Like McMahon, Downing recommended the use of fountains and cascades in the landscape. He felt that fountains were too little used in America and could add an interesting element to the landscape. As for sundials, he recommended them for use along walkways or as the center of a flower parterre. (figs. 26 & 27)

Downing achieved individuality in his landscape schemes by determining the plan through the study of "the nature and character of

Figures 26, 27. Downing advocated the placement of fountains and sundials within his gardens. He believed that they should be carefully integrated into the plan and not scattered on the lawn.

the scene." He took his cue from the land and the natural features themselves. And once he had determined the general areas for trees, ground and water, he then layed out his approach and walkways and added the necessary ornamentation. This is a very simple scheme, and it is still very useful today, both for reproducing an old garden and for laying out a new one.

The Essential Elements of an Early Nineteenth Century Landscape

Not everyone had a landscape in the fashion of A. J. Downing. As was mentioned earlier, on small lots, the ancient style was still used.

That scheme was also popular on country estates where there was no need to change, or where the owner was too conservative to change. Apparently, in conservative New England, although there were many landscapes in the Downing style, there were fewer in proportion to other parts of our new nation.

We can be quite certain, however, that if one were remodeling his house and landscape, the scheme he would have chosen would have been after Downing because of Downing's great influence. Many purchased his books, but even more subscribed to *The Horticulturist* where he put forth the same ideas. Other journals and builders' manuals were supporting the same concepts. Those who were reading McMahon and Loudon were obtaining much the same information.

If you are reproducing a landscape of the early nineteenth century, from your research, you must decide whether it should be the old ancient style or the "new fashion" of Downing. The essential characteristics of the former were set down earlier. Those for the latter are as follows:

1. As your house is already sited there is not very much you can do about that. However, you can restore the approach, either as a circular gravel drive or a cul-de-sac. Depressions in the grass, old drawings or pictures, or the location of old trees will often suggest the arrangement. (fig. 28)

2. If your property is very large, you will want to set out a belt of shrubs around the lawn area surrounding the house. If you are left with only a portion of the original property, the shrubs probably can only define the boundaries. Remember, Downing didn't like straight lines. These shrubs should be set out as shown in figures 19 or 22.

3. If there is room, you may want to include a belt walkway around the outside of the property but on the inside of the shrub border. Along the inside of the walk, you may wish to have some oval flower beds or an inner row of shrubs, broken with vistas towards the house.

4. Flower beds near the house should really be in period. If you do not have the time and energy to maintain beds of flowers, perhaps you could plant them with solid masses of groundcover that will not need much weeding. In this way, you will have a suggestion of flower beds but will not have to weed and water them.

5. Trees should be part of your plan. If you have a lawn area of several acres, away from the house, it would be ideal to plant this in the Downing style with masses of varied and picturesque trees and some single specimens too. If your property is small, then include some

Figure 28. A house in the gothic style. The depression in the lawn near the right corner of the house and the arrangement of the trees clearly indicate the location of a circular approach.

trees in informal groups to shade the house from the hot sun in summer or to informally enframe the driveway. Trees in a straight line should not be used with this style.

6. Don't use foundation plantings or a large, massed ribbon of shrubs along the foundation. The flower beds will be enough. If you really want a select shrub here or there, plant it, but do not repeat it with regularity. And remember, do not clutter the lawn with shrubs, as open lawns were the order of the day.

7. If your property is very small (maybe it always was) follow the concepts set forth in figure 22. You will note that the vegetable garden is in the rear, separated by a trellis (could be a shrub border) and an undulating flower bed. The foreground is lawn.

8. Add ornamentation in the form of cast iron or masonry vases (urns), sundials, and fountains. Downing advocated the placement of sundials on a pedestal or plinth; they should not be placed directly on the lawn without a base. He felt, and rightly so, that design-wise, these ornaments needed stability, or they would be lost visually. Urns should be associated with the house or other architectural structures, such as summerhouses. The same would be true of

55

fountains which look best placed either in the center of a parterre type garden or at the edge of a lawn area. Sundials were recommended for placement along a roundabout walk or as the focus for a garden, but they were not placed in the center of an open lawn.

Combinations of Styles

To think that all gardens were a pure expression of either the ancient or the natural style is a mistake. An older property, built in the seventeenth or eighteenth century, might have been "modernized" to include natural features, while retaining many of its old ones. At Mt. Vernon, Washington had an ancient type, wall enclosed, vegetable garden, as well as, a flower garden in the old style. (fig. 16) Yet he included many features in his revisions that were of the natural school.

The same would have been true in the gardens of lesser famous individuals. It is not likely that a productive garden in the ancient style, already walled. or fenced, would have been destroyed. But a meandering walkway through a grove of trees might be added on the site of an old orchard, for example, because of interest in the new style.

There were many examples of a combination of designs. Some estates had a very straight and majestic approach, such as Andrew Jackson's Hermitage. His wife's garden had many features of the ancient style. Yet other parts of the Hermitage landscape incorporated informal groupings of trees.

There were examples of gardens that employed some of Downing's principles but retained the noble approach drive. We can suppose that some individuals liked the majesty of a straight approach, lined with arching trees as opposed to a curvilinear, meandering approach with less forceful impact. The practice of planting trees along such an approach, or in adjoining groves, became quite popular as a means of commemorating an event such as a birth, the departure of a local, esteemed citizen for the War, or the return of a hero.

GARDENS OF PROSPERITY
1860 - 1900

The landscape style advocated by Downing prevailed throughout the nineteenth century. Numerous other authors reiterated his theories and expanded upon them between 1860 and 1900. Their works included only slight variations.

This type of garden design was considered "tasteful," and throughout the Victorian era, people "of taste" landscaped their grounds following the tenets of Repton and Loudon as expressed by Downing in America. Slightly more ornamentation was employed in the form of flower beds in varied shapes. Also, fountains and ornamental statues, such as deer and other animals, were placed to accent an entrance or break up a large lawn. But taste was always mentioned in most writings as being important. It consisted of creating a garden in keeping with the architecture of the house, providing a fine approach to the house, siting the house in a large lawn, and separating the service features (clothes drying, vegetable garden, barn, and orchard) from the rest of the landscape. It was also considered in good taste to plant a belt of trees and shrubs along the boundary and to separate functional spaces. (fig. 29)

The late nineteenth century was an era of prosperity. Technology had advanced rapidly, and wealth abounded for many, certainly for those who held high positions in the many factories and other growing enterprises. Agriculture was no longer the major occupation of American citizens. In fact, less than 50 percent of the population were engaged in farming as opposed to 94 percent in 1790. There were numerous plant expeditions and importations resulting in a plethora of exotic species for landscape use. Gardeners were anxious to try the many new species they read about in the newspapers and journals. Greenhouses, virtually non-existant 100 years earlier, were common, which meant that exotic plants could be wintered inside and planted outside in the summer. These were not only the golden years of technology, but also the golden years of horticulture.

Unless one showed great restraint, it was very easy to clutter his landscape with a variety of landscape features and styles covering many

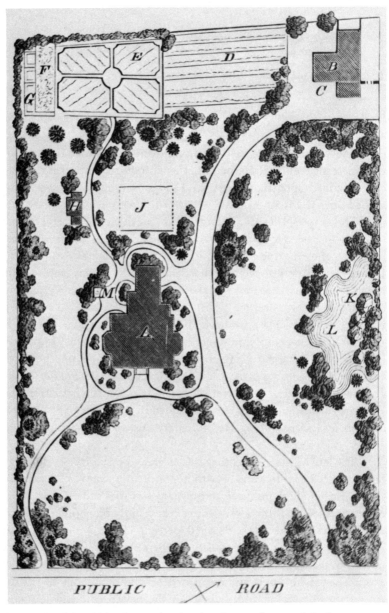

Figure 29. A late 19th century plan showing the use of trees and shrubs to separate spaces and to lend privacy.

Figure 30. Exaggerated form in attire as well as the garden.

Figure 31. A parterre in the 19th century manner where less restraint was shown in the use of plants and ornamentation.

periods. This eclectic type of garden design was certainly common where one's wealth transported him beyond the bounds of what was considered "good taste." Many writers warned against including too many features in the landscape, but some individuals could not resist.

One excellent writer of the period, Jacob Weidenmann (1829 - 1893), whose book *Beautifying Country Homes* was published in 1870, warned against duplicating the same ornaments in the same landscape too many times and recommended the use of restraint both in the landscape styles used and in ornamentation. Yet, in another passage, he advocates using hollowed tree stumps planted with annual flowers as an ornament in the garden.

This was an era of exaggeration, mainly of form, styles, and ornament. Exaggeration prevailed in the facial hirsute of males, the attire of both men and women, in the architecture of houses, in the design of buggies and carriages, in the design of benches, seats and other garden ornaments. Even the plant material used consisted of exaggerated form: dwarf, over-sized, weeping, strict-erect, variegated, colored, and large-leaved forms. (fig. 30)

Technology spurred this concept along. While the practice of casting iron was ancient, it could now be mass produced into fences, urns, benches, hitching posts, deer for the lawn and fountains. Labor for turning out these ornaments was inexpensive and money was no object.

The Era of Eclecticism

While some gardens retained the design concepts of the early nineteenth century, others took features from several different periods and put them together in one landscape. It was not uncommon to find in one garden long, wide, axial vistas, rigidly framed by trees, with the center foreground containing a long, linear pool, quite reminiscent of the French style. Entrances to properties were enriched with noble pilasters and gates, which added an air of majesty to the landscape.

The French parterre also enjoyed a revival during this era, and all kinds of variations were made upon it. Some parterres were executed with restraint, but others were filled with flowers, roses, and a variety of colorful plant material. (fig. 31)

Elements were taken from Italian gardens as well. Statuary of all kinds, cast iron, as well as, marble and stone, found its way into the garden. Much of it was in the form of animals, but some was classical in nature. Fountains, also, were more commonly installed, and many of them were highly complex. One such fountain, for example, had water spouting from a swan's neck while little cherubs danced in the pool below. (fig. 32)

Another Italian feature employed was the balustraded terrace. Terraces connected by steps were edged with elaborate balustrades just like the famous Renaissance gardens in Italy. No restraint was shown in the use of plant material, and the terrace gardens of the Victorian era abounded with colorful plants. Columnar trees, quite like the cypress of Italy, were planted for accent throughout the garden.

Classical garden styles were also revived. Columns of marble were imported for use as accents, background for the garden, or as supports for pergolas. Statues of Greek gods frequently made their appearance in the gardens. Of course, classical urns or vases continued to be popular, but during the later years of this century, they were often filled with flowers rather than left empty as a sculptural element.

Oriental features found their way into the Victorian garden. Summer houses built in the oriental style were very popular as were oriental bridges, built over streams and brooks. Sometimes an oriental garden was built which meant that an entire natural landscape had been recreated and telescoped into a small place. (fig. 33)

Formal gardens of various styles: French, Italian, Classical, or

Figure 32. Various types of garden ornament. Motifs that showed exaggerated form and sinuous lines were selected.

Figure 33. A summerhouse in the oriental style.

Ancient were the order of the day. Except for a few who followed the advice of early authors, such as, Downing, Weidenmann, and their successors, most people planted their gardens in one or more of the formal styles.

It was considered bad taste to mix a variety of styles in one garden, but it was done to some extent. There were gardens that contained "one of everything," so to speak. Classical urns, cast iron statues, Doric columns, parterres, and topiary might all appear in one garden. Few writers of the period recommended this, but of course not everyone who installed a garden read books.

Ornamental Features

One feature that practically every garden contained was a fence. They were recommended as definition for the boundary of the property, to prevent intrusion, and as an ornament. Even in the late nineteenth century, most properties were fenced because, in many communities, various forms of livestock still roamed the street.

Unless the fence was used as an ornament, it was recommended that it be hidden from view by shrubs. This idea was probably a holdover from the days when the ha-ha was introduced because fences were considered ugly. Picket fences were thought to be quite old fashioned, stiff, and unnatural. This fence, that once was so popular, was now considered passé. (fig. 34)

Iron fences, though more costly, were the ideal and were to be used whenever possible. Obviously, they were most ornamental because patterns could be cast in an infinite variety. As one travels throughout this country, it is interesting to note the many different designs of cast iron fences. Similarities may occur within a particular region because the local foundry created and cast its own patterns. (fig. 35)

Hedges were not recommended for garden enclosure. If there was need for shelter or screening, then hedges were advocated, but otherwise they were not considered ornamental enough to act as an enclosure, perhaps due to their rigidity. In the early twentieth century, however, hedges again became more popular.

There were a variety of ornamental features used in the garden that were related to sitting. Chairs, benches, and sitting pavillions were extensively used. These furnishings were constructed of wood and cast iron. Chairs and benches were built for ornament as well as comfort. Obviously, a cast iron bench consisting of involved filigree of grapes and vines could not have been very comfortable as a seat, nor could benches built of rustic branches. But not all garden seats were

Figure 34. 19th century wooden fences showing intricate designs.

Figure 35. Cast iron lent itself to the creation of highly ornamented patterns.

66

made so highly ornamented, and many were simple and comfortable. (See figure 32.)

On high rises of ground, pavillions were built. These were covered seats and usually situated to gain a prospect of the surrounding garden and countryside. We might say that they were an evolved version of the ancient mounts built in gardens where a tower was so sited upon a mound that one could see beyond the garden wall. Garden pavillions were often planted with vines that grew up a trellis and onto their roofs. (See figure 13.)

Statues or sculpture of various sorts adorned most gardens. Even the earliest garden designers recommended the use of vases or urns set upon an appropriate base or plinth. But in the late nineteenth century, other sculptural elements entered the garden. Animal motifs, in stone, marble and especially cast iron, were popular. Often they were used at the entrances to the garden, but many owners set them about on their lawns as well, in spite of the fact that garden writers advised against this practice because it tended to clutter and create a nuisance for lawn mowing. (See figure 32.)

Early in the nineteenth century, Downing had agreed with Loudon that urns or vases should not be planted with flowers. But in the late Victorian era, most urns were planted with flowers, and drooping vines were set along the edge of the urn for a cascading effect. In fact, urns were built out of wood in the rustic style and placed about on the lawn and on porches. (fig. 36)

Sundials, popular landscape features for centuries, became even more popular during the late nineteenth century. They often formed the focus for rose or perennial gardens designed as parterres. Sometimes, they were placed in a round bed on the lawn or preferably placed in a garden on the edge of the lawn.

Shrubs, Trees, and Garden Flowers

Shade trees continued in popularity as landscape features and were planted to enframe an approach to the house, along the street, or in informal groupings around the house. Specimen trees, especially weeping forms, were planted on the lawn, either in front or to the rear of the house. Trees were also set out along the boundaries of the property where sunlight was not important.

Shrubs were planted in masses along the boundary of the property, not very different from the scheme recommended by Downing in the early part of the nineteenth century. They were also massed at the juncture of walkways, and as background groupings for flower beds

Figure 36. A rustic plant stand made of wood. These were either placed on the lawn or on porches.

Figure 37. A late 19th century house showing a heavy foundation planting and carpet bedding in front.

and garden sculpture. Informal masses were planted on the lawn to separate various portions of the yard.

Less restraint was used in the selection of species and varieties than in previous years. By this time, there were many nurseries all promoting the latest plant introductions from the Orient and other parts of the globe. The selection was virtually unlimited. One could have every shape and form of shrub in practically any color or variegation.

Foundation plantings, the practice of girding the foundation of a house with shrubs, became common in the latter part of this period as house foundations were built taller and higher off the ground. Varieties of plants in various colors and forms, from round to conical, were planted together. Plants stood out as individuals, rather than blending together. (fig. 37)

American gardens had never enjoyed a greater era for variety in flowers. There were many varieties from which to choose and gardeners were selecting a few of each. Downing's advice (to use masses of one or two kinds of flowers in a bed) was not generally heeded. Instead, intricate mixtures were planted in a variety of designs.

69

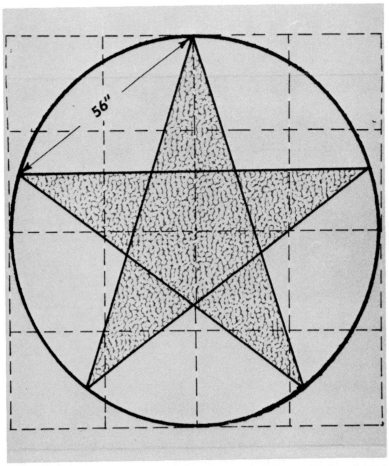

56"

Figure 38. Carpet bedding was revived in the Bicentennial celebration of 1976. Many organizations distributed plans for setting out flowers in patriotic designs.

Carpet bedding became very popular especially in parks. Gardeners would copy the designs they saw, though often their plantings were less involved and extensive. In carpet bedding, plants of all the same height were planted in very intricate designs. Some resembled mosaics, others, the webbing on a butterfly's wing, and one's imagination could really run wild. Plants for carpet beds were greenhouse grown and groomed so that all would be of the same height and vigor. One can imagine how time consuming these beds were to plant, lay out and care for, and how expensive the quantities of plants would be today. But, in those days, labor and materials were inexpensive. (See figures 37 & 38.)

70

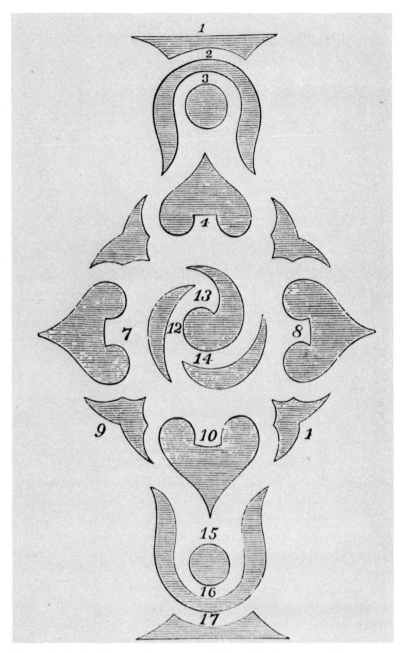

Figure 39. A plan for a rosarium patterned after a French parterre design.

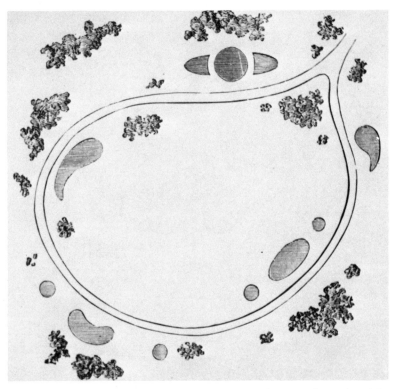

Figure 40. A plan showing the placement of flower borders around the edge of the lawn.

Most beds in the lawn were round or oval; some were square or rectangular. Still others were arabesques, meaning that they were sinuous and curved. Carpet beds were so situated that they would either be seen from the public way or from the busiest rooms of the house. Often they were planted on an inclined slope for more dramatic display.

Rosariums were very important during this era and often planted in hedged parterres or in many-parted gardens. Often climbing roses were grown over a pavillion or arched trellises in the center. The outer beds contained shrub roses. Sometimes the garden was edged with climbing roses on trellises. It was not uncommon to see the paths of the garden arched with climbing roses at intervals. (fig. 39)

Perennial gardens were as popular as rosariums during this era. As with other plants, many new varieties of perennials had been bred and

Figure 41. A wild garden or the practice of planting flowers much as they would grow in nature.

introduced and, therefore, lavishly planted in the landscape. Perennial gardens were either planted in many parted beds, as were roses, or they were planted in borders around the edge of the lawn. The former style was the most popular. (fig. 40)

The Gay Nineties and the Early Twentieth Century

Perennial borders became very popular during this period. The influence of the Englishman William Robinson (1839 - 1933), who detested bedding out and involved garden designs, was being felt. Robinson advocated the planting of large, deep perennial beds. Depths exceeding a ten foot minimum were recommended, and within these borders, masses of perennials were to be planted in an organized and designed manner. Robinson's ideas were also being recommended by many American garden writers and designers, and his concepts were readily accepted.

Robinson also advocated wild gardens and woodland walks where flowers were planted in a woodland setting along a path or walk. These gardens became very popular on large estates in the early part of the twentieth century, and they were even copied on smaller scale landscapes. (fig. 41)

73

As the nineteenth century drew to a close and the twentieth century emerged, eclecticism began to give way to a crisp and clear expression of just one or two styles within a landscape. For example, houses might be built in the English Tudor style and surrounded by a garden of the same period. The outskirts of the property might contain a woodland walk. Or, another individual might build an Italian garden surrounding his house of a related period, and this too might be surrounded by an informal shrub or flower garden associated with informal groupings of trees.

Essential Characteristics of Gardens of Prosperity

On the surface, it might appear that gardens of this era are virtually impossible to recreate, given the high cost of materials and labor. But, even though these gardens were very involved, it is possible to incorporate their essential characteristics into a garden that will generate the feeling of the late nineteenth century.

1. Lawn - These gardens had large front and rear lawns, although in some cases where sites were small, front and side yards were narrow and rear yards large. In any event, lawns were basic.

2. Trees - Within the lawn area specimen trees were important. These were planted to cast shade upon important parts of the house and yard and also to enframe the house and the drive or approach. Often trees were placed along the street.

   Weeping trees and those with variegated or colored foliage were popular and common. Not all the trees should be weeping or variegated or colored, but certain strategic ones should.

3. Shrubs - If your house is of the late nineteenth century with a very high foundation, a foundation planting might be in order. Taller plants were placed at the corner of the house and shorter plants in between. Accent plants were planted to enframe the doorway, turrets, or bay windows.

   Shrubs also were planted at the juncture of walks and along the property lines. A mixture of species was very popular.

4. Fencing - Most, if not all, properties of this period were fenced. Cast iron fencing is difficult to obtain, but often it is available through used material dealers. If it is impossible to obtain, wood fencing, highly ornamented, should be substituted.

5. Ornaments - Urns and garden sculpture, including sundials should be incorporated into the scheme. It is not essential to have an abundance of these materials. In fact it was not considered good taste to do so. However, a few good pieces, placed as indicated

previously in this chapter, are in order. Urns and fountains are not difficult to purchase through used materials and antique dealers.

6. Benches, seats, and pavillions - Cast iron benches as well as wooden ones are not difficult to find and are easily placed in the garden as focal points or under trees. Garden pavillions, though decorative and picturesque, are expensive to build and are not entirely necessary to complete the scheme.

7. Flowers - While flowers were an essential part of the late nineteenth century landscape, some may find them difficult to maintain. Certainly, carpet bedding would be hard to keep up and very costly to install. However, a few circular beds, on either side of the front walk, are not difficult, and if massed solid with plants and carefully mulched, they are easy to keep weed free.

8. Vines - Vines on fences and trellises are decorative, and they provide the proper late nineteenth century atmosphere. Most vines do not require a lot of attention. Mainly they require some clipping at least once each year. The very rampant ones may require some additional treatment.

GARDENS OF CRAFTSMEN
AND WORKMEN
1800 - 1900

Gardens of craftsmen and workmen were rarely ornamented unless the woman of the household had a particular interest in flowers. The gardens of individuals of this way of life consisted more of a place to grow vegetables rather than a beautiful display of ornamental plants and landscape features.

In the early nineteenth century, many Americans went to work in a shop or one of the small mills that were cropping up along rivers and streams. Agriculture was no longer the primary way of life. Land was sold off and smaller plots encircled the houses of the workman and craftsman.

Plots were set aside for vegetables, and flowers were usually grown in the dooryard immediately between the street and the house or near the rear door, whichever was the sunniest spot. Or, simple flower beds were placed along the fence which enclosed the yard. Vegetable gardens were usually to the rear of the house, while flower gardens were placed nearer the public way where they might be seen. (fig. 42)

Shrubbery and trees, including fruit trees, were often placed along the borders of the property or placed in such a way to shade certain portions of the yard where outdoor activities such as washing and soap-making were performed. Consideration was also given to cutting down the rays of the sun to make the house more comfortable in summer.

As the nineteenth century progressed, most wives of workmen and craftsmen attempted to enrich their properties with the same kinds of landscape features that adorned wealthier estates. Round beds often accented the front walk, one on either side. Or a large round bed, planted with dahlias or cannas, might be sited in a side lawn. Urns were placed in the lawn, but few gardens could afford sundials or sculpture. Weeping mulberries and clipped catalpas were often used as substitutes. Meandering walks, drives or magnificent approaches to the house were unheard of because usually the property was not extensive enough, and funds were not available for upkeep. Cast iron

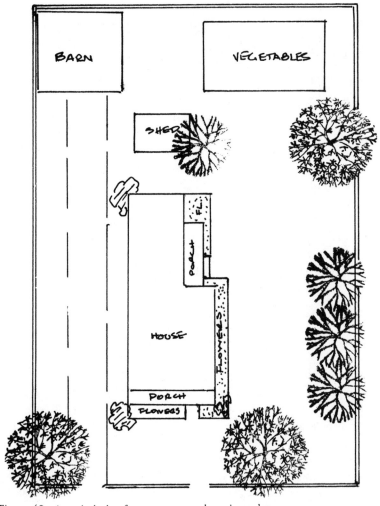

Figure 42. A typical plan for a country workman's garden.

fences were often used along the boundaries, but wooden fences were most common.

The following description was the most typical plan, and the one that prevailed right into this century. The house was sited quite near the front of a small lot. A front yard, consisting of a shade tree, lawn, and some shrubs planted along the foundation, formed the entrance

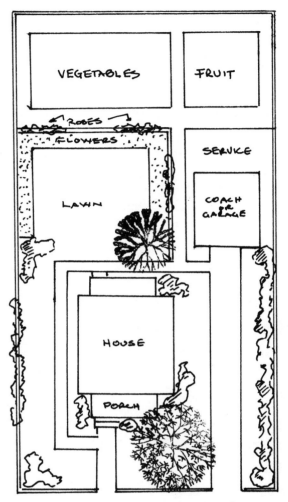

VEGETABLES

FRUIT

ROSES

FLOWERS

SERVICE

LAWN

COACH or GARAGE

HOUSE

PORCH

Figure 43. A typical plan for a town or city workman's garden.

space. A drive along one side of the house led to a barn, shop and later a garage. The rear yard, immediately behind the house, often consisted of a grass panel in the center, encircled by a flower garden and shrubs. This yard tripled for sitting, playing, and clothes drying. The very rear of the property was devoted to vegetables. When the rear yard was very small, its entirety was usually planted with vegetables. (fig. 43)

79

AUTHENTIC PLANTS
1620 - 1900

In reproducing a period landscape, it is not enough to lay out the garden in an appropriate and authentic design. Each era had its own style of plants, and it is important to select those that will create the desired effect.

In the colonial period, or specifically, before the Revolutionary War, there were not many nurseries. Plants were limited and very often were exchanged from one gardener to the other, imported from abroad, or native plants were used. After we became a nation, plant explorations were encouraged, more plants were imported, and many nurseries were established. This meant that a greater variety of plants were readily available for use by all.

After the Revolution, greater attention was paid to the use of trees in the landscape as part of the emergence of the natural style. Ornamental varieties became very popular, and evergreens were intermixed with non evergreens. Before this time, except for an occasional shade tree, trees were considered utilitarian, but by the early nineteenth century they were thought of as ornamental as well.

As the wealth of the nation increased, greater emphasis was placed on the use of flowers and other ornaments in the landscape. It became important to set off one's house with an extensive lawn, tastefully darted with oval beds of flowers. With this increased attention placed on annuals and perennials, more species and varieties were bred and introduced.

As the nineteenth century unfolded, the older flowers went out of style. In fact, such flowers as Hollyhocks, Sunflowers, Daylilies, Gilliflowers, Poppies, Nasturtiums, Larkspurs, Snapdragons, Pansies, and Seathrift were considered old-fashioned and often referred to as being appropriate for a "grandmother's garden." (fig. 44)

In their place, large and bold foliaged plants or those with a definite shape or form were recommended. Lilies were suddenly very popular and many new ones were being introduced from the Orient. Castor Beans were planted in the center of large beds. Cannas, dahlias

Figure 44. A "grandmother's garden" where old-fashioned flowers were grown in a quaint style.

and other large-flowered plants replaced hollyhocks and larkspurs. Ornamental grasses were very popular. (fig. 45)

The following list contains popular plants for particular eras. They represent the plants known to have been grown during the years designated. Where particular plants were popular during an earlier era as well, they are marked with an asterisk.

AUTHENTIC PLANTS FOR RESTORING AND REPRODUCING PERIOD LANDSCAPES

FLOWERS - 1600-1699

Achillea millefolium	Yarrow
Aconitum napellus	Aconitum, Wolfsbane
Althaea rosea	Hollyhock, Garden or French Mallows, "single, double and several colors"
Amaranthus caudatus	Love-lies-bleeding, Tassel Flower, Flower Gentle, "used by country women"
Amaranthus tricolor	Tri-color Amaranth or Joseph's Coat
Anemone coronaria, probably	Anemone, tuberous types
Anemone pulsatilla	Pasque Flower, Windflower or Emanies
Antirrhinum majus	Snapdragon, "red, white, purple, variable"

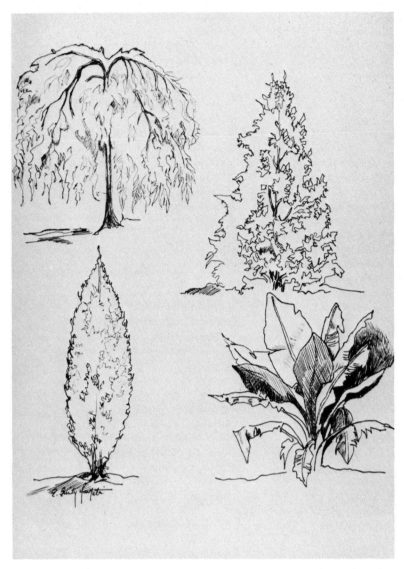

Figure 45. Bold-form plants — weeping, strict-erect, conical and large-leaved.

Aquilegia sp.	Columbine, "singles and doubles"
Asphodelus albus	Asphodell
Asphodelus luteus	Asphodell or King's Spear
Aster sp.	Aster, Starwort
Bellis perennis	English Daisy, Herb Margaret, Ewe - or May-gowan, Childing Daisy, Bone - or Bruisewort, Bone Flower, March Daisy, Bairnwort
Calendula officinalis	Calendula, "Pot Marygold"
Campanula medium	Canterbury Bells, "doubles"
Campanula persicifolia	Bellflower
Centaurea sp., probably	Centaury
Centaurea cyanus	Cornflower, Blew Bottle
Chelidonicum majus	Celandine Poppy
Chieranthus cheiri	Wallflower, "keiri"
Chrysanthemum leucanthemum (possibly) or Bellis perennis	Daisies
Chrysanthemum parthenium	Feverfew, Fether-few
Colchicum autumnale, var. atropurpureum	Colchichum, Meadow Saffron
Convallaria majalis	Lily-of-the-valley
Convolvulus sp.	Convolvulus, Bindweed, Blew Bindweed, or Morning Glory, a modern name
Crocus vernus	Crocus, "white, small purple, large purple, yellow"
Cucurbita pepo var. ovifera, probably	Gourds
Datura stramonium	Thornapple or Jimson Weed
Delphinium ajacis	Larkspur, Delphinium or Larks Heels
Dianthus barbatus	Sweet William, Armeria, Sweet John
Dianthus sp.	Clove, Gilliflowers or Pinks, "red and white, pink and white"
Dictamnus albus	Dittany or Fraxinella
Digitalis purpurea	Foxglove
Epimedium sp. probably alpinum or grandiflorum	Epimedium or Barrenwort
Eranthis hyemalis	Winter Aconite
Eryngium maritimum	Sea Holly
Erythronium dens-canis	Dogtooth Violet, "Dens-caninus"
Fritillaria imperalis	Crown Imperial
Fritillaria meleagris	Chequered Lily
Geranium maculatum, robertianum or lancastriense, probably	Cranesbill, Geranium, "blue, white, and rose"
Gladiolus sp.	Gladiolus or Corn Flag
Gomphrena globosa	Globe Amaranth, Batchelors Button
Helianthus annuus, probably	Sunflower, "very tall"
Helichrysum bracteatum	Strawflower or Everlasting
Helleborous niger	Helleborous, "the black flower at Christmas"

Hemerocallis flava	Yellow Daylily
Hemerocallis fulva	Tawny Daylily
Iberis umbellata, probably	Candytuft
Hepatica sp.	Hepatica, Liver-worts
Hesperis matronalis	Rocket or Dames Violet
Hyacinthus sp.	Hyacinth or Jacenths
Impatiens balsamina	Balsam
Innula helenium	Elecampane
Iris germanica var. florentina alba	Iris
Iris praecox	Bulbous Iris
Iris sp.	Iris, "flower-de-luce", flags, blue and varied"
Iris susiana	Mourning Iris, referred to as "turkish", bulbous
Iris variegata, could also apply to striped-leaved forms of other Irises	Iris
Iris xiphiodes	English Iris, bulbous
Lamium sp., probably maculatum, album or purpureum	Dead Nettle
Lathyrus latifolius	Perennial Sweet Pea
Leucojum vernum	Great Spring Snowdrop
Lilium auratum, L. martagon or L. speciosum var. album	White Lily
Lilium canadense	Meadow Lily
Lilium martagon	Martagon or Turks-Cap Lily
Linaria sp.	Toad Flax, Wild Flax
Lobelia cardinalis	Cardinal Flower
Lupinus sp.	Lupine
Lychnis chalcedonica	Lychnis, Maltese Cross, or Red Campion
Lychnis coronaria	Lychnis, Nonesuch, Flower of Bristow, Constantinople, Flower of Bristol
Lycopersicum esculentum	Tomato or "pomum amoris", always listed as an ornamental during this period
Mathiola incana	Gilliflower, Stock-Gilliflower or Wallflower
Mimosa pudica	Sensitive Plant
Mirabilis jalapa	Mirabilis, Four-o'cloks, or Marvel of Peru
Monarda fistulosa	Blue Monarda
Muscari botryoides	Grape Hyacinth
Narcissus sp.	Daffodils, Daffadown Dillies, "trumpets, poets, doubles or multiplex"
Nepeta hederacea	Ground Ivy, Ale-hoof
Nigella damascena	Nigella, or Fennel Flower
Ornithogallum umbellatum	Star-of-Bethlehem
Paeonia officinalis	Peony, "double red, double purple"

Papaver sp.	French Double Poppy, "ornaments of the garden", "red, scarlet, lead color, white, blush"
Parietoria officinalis	Pelletory
Physalis alkekengi	Alkenkengi, Winterberry, Winter-Cherry or Chinese Lantern Plant
Primula auricula	Primroses, Cowslips, Beare's Ears, Oxslips, "purple, purple & yellow, sable, red, yellow, white"
Pulmonaria angustifolia	Lungwort
Ranunculus acris, probably	Crowsfoot, Ranunculus, Fair Maids of France, "has escaped to the wild"
Ranunculus asiatius	Garden Ranunculus, Turban or Persian
Ranunculus creticus	Creten Ranunculus
Sanguinaria canadensis	Bloodroot, Puckoon
Scabiosa atropurpurea	Scabiosa, "White and Red"
Tagetes sp.	Marygold
Tagetes erecta	African Marigold or "Flos Africanis" or "Flos Africanis Multiplex"
Tagetes patula	French Marigold - Note: While both the so-called African and French Marigolds were grown, it appears from the literature that what we know today as French Marigolds were most common. In fact, it appears that the names, African & French were used loosely to apply to T. patula. The issue is further confused in that Calendula (C. officinalis) was also called "Marygold".
Taraxacum officinale	Dandelion, Leontodon
Teucrium chamaedrys	Germander
Thalictrum aquilegifolium	Meadow Rue, Feathered Columbine
Tropaeolum majus	Nasturtium, or Indian Cress, Often listed as an herb or vegetable because it was eaten (leaves and buds).
Tulipa sp.	Tulips, Mainly broken types grown. Also "doubles and singles"
Valeriana officinalis or Polemonium caeruleum	Valerian, Jacob's Ladder
Verbascum thapsis, probably	Verbascum, Mullein or Moth Mullein
Viola sp.	Violets
Viola tricolor	Pansy or Heart's Ease
Yucca filamentosa	Yucca

SHRUBS, TREES, AND VINES - 1600-1699

Abies sp.	Fir
Acer rubrum	Red Maple
Buxus sempervirens	English Box
Campsis radicans	Trumpet Flower
Celtis occidentalis	Hackberry, American Nettle-tree

Cercis canadensis	Red-bud, Arbor-Judae, Judas Tree or Sallad Tree
Cornus amomum	Silky Dogwood
Cornus florida	Dogwood
Cornus mas	Cornelian Cherry or Cornel
Cornus stolonifera	Red Osier Dogwood
Cotinus coggygria	Smoke Tree or Venetian sumach
Cytisus multiflorus	Spanish Cytisus, White Spanish Broom
Daphne mezereum	Mezereum, Chamelaea
Filipendula hexapetala, probably	Spirea or Dropwort, Most spireas were not introduced until later, but the Filipendulas were called Spireas at this time.
Gelsemium sempervirens	Honeysuckle, Carolina Yellow Jessamine, Jasmine
Hamamelis virginiana	Witch Hazel
Hibiscus syriacus	Althaea, Rose-of-Sharon
Hypericum densiflorum	Bushy Saint John's Wort
Hypericum sp., possibly Hypericum calycinum	Hypericum, St. John's Wort
Ilex glabra, probably or Ilex verticillata	Winterberry, This name sometimes refers to Physalis alkekengi.
Ilex sp.	Holly
Jasminum sambac	Jasmine, Arabian Pipe
Juniperus sabina	Savin Tree or Bush, Savine or Sabin Juniper
Juniperus virginiana	Juniper, Cedar, Red Cedar or Eastern Red Cedar
Laburnum anagyroides	Common Laburnum, Golden-chain or Beantree
Lantana camara	Lantana, for indoor culture
Larix decidua, probably	Larch
Ligustrum vulgare	Common Privet, Primworth, Skedge or Skedgewirth
Lindera benzoin	Spicebush
Liquidambar styraciflua	Sweet Gum
Liriodendron tulipifera	Tulip Tree
Lonicera periclymenum	Honeysuckle, French Honeysuckle, Red-Satin Flower, Woodbine, Common English Honeysuckle
Lonicera sempervirens	Honeysuckle, Scarlet or French, or Coral
Magnolia virginiana	Magnolia, Sweet Bay, Swamp Magnolia or Bay Laurel
Myrica pennsylvanica	Bayberry or Wax Myrtle, Candleberry Myrtle
Parthenocissus quinquefolia	Virginia Creeper
Periploca graeca, probably	Periploca
Philadelphus coronarius	Mock Orange, Syringa, Pipe Tree, see Syringa vulgaris
Pinus sp.	Pine

Platanus occidentalis	Sycamore, Plane-Tree or Large Buttonwood
Platanus orientalis	Oriental Plane Tree
Populus sp.	Poplar
Prunus serotina	Wild Cherry
Pyracantha coccinea, probably	Pyracantha or Coral Tree
Quercus alba	White Oak
Quercus borealis	Red Oak, Quercus rubra in literature
Quercus coccinea	Scarlet Oak
Robinia pseudoacacia	Locust
Rosa canina	Dog Rose
Rosa centifolia	Cabbage Rose
Rosa damascena	Damask Rose
Rosa damascena var. versicolor	York and Lancaster Rose
Rosa eglanteria	Rose, Sweet Briar, Eglantine
Rosa gallica	French Rose
Rosa gallica var. versicolor	Rosamundi Rose
Rosa moschata	Musk Rose
Rosa pomifera	Apple Rose
Rosa sempervirens, probably	Evergreen Rose
Sassafras albidum	Sassafras
Sorbus domestica or torminalis	Service Tree or Sorbus, "liked as a fruit tree"
Staphylea pinnata, probably	Bladder-nut, "beareth sweet whitish flowers"
Syringa vulgaris or Philadelphus coronarius	Syringa, Pipe Tree, Lilac - In 1597 John Gerarde in his "Herball" calls Philadelphus a Syringa or "White Pipe Tree"; he also calls the lilac "Blue Pipe". The name Pipe Tree comes from the fact that pith can be removed from the stem of Philadelphus leaving a hollow receptacle that was made into a pipe.
Thuja occidentalis	Arbor-vitae or Northern White Cedar
Tilia sp. probably platyphyllos or europa	Linden or Lime
Viburnum opulus var. roseum	Guelder Rose or Gelder - Other viburnums also called by this common name, but it seems to have been most associated with this species.
Tsuga canadensis	Canada Hemlock or Pine or Fir Hemlock

VEGETABLES AND FIELD CROPS - 1600-1699

Allium cepa	Onion
Allium porrum	Leeks
Allium sativum	Garlic
Asparagus officinalis	Asparagus
Avena sativa	Oats
Beta vulgaris	Beet
Brassica oleracea var. capitata	Cabbage, Savoy - The variety Savoy is mentioned repeatedly and is still available today.

88

Brassica oleracea var.	
botrytis	Cauliflower, Cole-flower
Brassica rapa	Turnip
Campanula rapunculus	Rampion
Cannabis sativa	Hemp
Cicorium intybus	Wild Endive, Succory
Citrullus vulgaris	Melon
Cucumis melo	Musk Melon
Cucumis sativus	Cucumber
Cucurbita pepo	Pumpkin, Pompion
Cucurbita sp.	Squash
Cynara scolymus	Artichoke
Daucus carota	Carrot
Helianthus tuberosus	Jerusalem Artichoke
Hordeum vulgare	Barley
Humulus lupulus	Hops
Lactuca sativa	Lettuce
Nicotiana tabacum	Tobacco
Pastinaca sativa	Parsnip
Petroselinum crispum	Parsley
Phaseolus vulgaris	Bean
Pisum sativum	Pea
Raphanus sativus	Radish
Secale cereale	Rye
Solanum tuberosum	Potato
Spinacia oleracea	Spinach
Triticum aestivum	Wheat
Zea mays	Corn, "Corne", Maize

FRUITS AND NUTS - 1600-1699

Berberis vulgaris	Barberry, Oxycantha or Berberry
Citrus aurantium	Orange
Corylus americana	Hazel or Hazelnut
Corylus maxima	Filberts or Bilbeards
Cydonia oblonga	Quince
Ficus carica	Fig
Fragaria virginiana	Strawberry
Juglans sp.	Walnut
Malus pumila - hybrid derivations	
from this species	Apple
Mespilus germanica	Medlar
Morus sp.	Mulberry
Prunus armeniaca	Apricot or Apricock
Prunus cerasus	Cherry, Sour Cherry
Prunus amygdalus	Almond
Prunus domestica	Plum - "white, red, blue, being almost as good as the Damson
Prunus persica	Peach

Prunus persica var. nectarina	Nectarine
Punica granatum	Pomegranate
Pyrus communis	Pear or Peare
Ribes grossularia	Gooseberry
Ribes sativum	Currant
Rubus idaeus	Raspberry
Sambucus canadensis	Elderberry or Eldern
Vitis vinifera	Grapes, "white and red, blew, muscadine"

HERBS - AROMATIC, CULINARY AND MEDICINAL - 1600-1776

Achillea millefolium	Yarrow
Allium schoenoprasium	Chives, Chibbals, Cives
Anchusa sempervirens	Alkanet, Bugloss
Anethum graveolens	Dill
Angelica archangelica	Angelica
Anthemis nobilis	Chamomille
Anthriscus cerefolium	Chervil
Artemisia abrotanum	Southernwood
Artemisia dracunculus	Tarragon
Borago officinalis	Borage
Brassica, probably juncea	Mustard
Calendula officinalis	Calendula, Marygold, Pot Marygold
Carum carvi	Caraway
Chrysanthemum balsamita	Costmary, Bibleleaf
Coriandrum sativum	Coriander
Crocus sativus	Saffron
Foeniculum vulgare	Fennel
Glycyrrhiza glabra	Licorice, Liquorice
Hyssopus officinalis	Hyssop, Isop
Isatis tinctoria	Woad, Weld or Dyer's Woad
Lavandula officinalis	Lavender
Lepidium sativum	Cress
Levisticum officinale	Lovage
Linum usitatissimum	Flax
Melissa officinalis	Balm
Mentha sp.	Mints, Garden Mints, "divers sorts"
Mentha spicata	Spearmint
Myrrhis odorata	Sweet Cicely
Nepeta cataria	Catmint, Catnip
Nicotiana tabacum, Nicotiana rustica	Tobacco
Ocimum basilicum	Basil
Ophrys apifera	Bee-flower
Petroselinium crispum var. latifolium	Parsley
Pimpinella anisum	Anise
Portulaca oleracea	Purslane

Rheum rhaponticum	Rhubarb
Rosmarinus officinalis	Rosemary
Rubia tinctorum	Madder
Rumex acetosa	Sorrel
Rumex probably patientia	Dock
Ruta graveolens	Rue
Salvia officinalis	Sage
Salvia sclarea	Clary
Sanguisorba officinalis	Burnett
Santolina chamaecyparissus	Santolina, or Lavender Cotton
Satureja, probably both hortensis and montana	Savory
Sempervivum tectorum, probably	Houseleek
Sisum sisarum	Skirret
Symphytum officinale	Comfrey
Tanacetum vulgare	Tansy
Thymus serpyllum	Thyme, Time

FLOWERS - 1700-1776

Adiantum pedatum	Maidenhair Fern
Anaphalis margaritacea	Everlasting Flowers or Pearl Everlasting
Aquilegia canadensis	Columbine
Arctostaphylos uva-ursi	Bear Berry
Argemone grandiflora	Prickly Poppy
Callistephus chinensis	China Aster
Celosia argentea, Celosia argentea var. cristata, Celosia argentea var. plumosa	Cockscomb
Chelone glabra	Turtlehead
Coreopsis lanceolata	Coreopsis, Tickseed
Delphinium ajacis or consolida	Larkspur or Delphinium
Dianthus caryophyllus	Carnations
Dianthus plumarius	Grass Pinks, Cottage Pink
Draba verna	Whitlow Grass
Galanthus nivalis	Snowdrop
Galax aphylla	Galix
Gallium luteum	Yellow Bedstraw
Geranium maculatum	Crane's-bill
Geranium robertianum	Crane's-bill, Herb-Robert or Red Robin
Helianthus annuus	Sunflower
Hibiscus moscheutos	Rose Mallow
Hyacinthus orientalis	Purple Hyacinth
Hypericum linarifolium	Flax-leaved St. John's Wort
Impatiens balsamina	Balsam, "double"
Iris cristata	Dwarf Iris
Iris pallida	Iris - one of the most important sources of tall bearded irises of gardens.
Iris pseudacorus	Yellow Iris

Lathyrus maritimus	Beach Pea
Lathyrus odoratus	Annual Sweet Pea
Lunaria annua	Lunaria, Moonwort, Honesty
Lychnis dioica	Catchfly, Morning Campion, Red Campion
Lychnis viscaria	Catchfly, German Catchfly
Lysimachia nummularia	Creeping Jenny, Creeping Charley, Moneywort
Mertensia virginica	Virginia Bluebells
Monarda didyma	Bee Balm
Muscari comosum var.	
monstrosum	Feathered Hyacinth
Narcissus jonquilla	Narcissus or Jonquil
Narcissus poeticus	Poets Narcissus
Oenothera biennis	Evening Primrose
Paeonia suffruticosa	Tree Peony
Papaver orientale	Oriental Poppy
Phlox divaricata	Blue Phlox
Phlox glaberrima	Phlox
Phlox maculata	Phlox
Phlox paniculata	Summer Phlox or Lychnidea
Poa agrostis	Bent Grass
Primula vulgaris	English Primroses
Rudbeckia hirta	Black-eyed Susan
Saponaria officinalis	Bouncing Bet, Soapwort
Saururus cernuus	Lizard's Tail
Scilla hispanica	Squill, Spanish Bluebell
Scilla sibirica	Siberian Squill
Senecio aureus	Golden Ragwort
Sternbergia lutea	Fall Daffodil - By 1806 the common name of Yellow Amaryllis is also used.
Stokesia laevis	Stokes Aster
Tiarella cordifolia	Foamflower
Trollius asiaticus	Trollius
Typha latifolia	Cat-tail
Valeriana officinalis	Valerian
Verbena officinalis	Vervain
Veronica maritima or longifolia	Veronica
Vinca minor	Periwinkle
Viola canadensis, cucullata, hastata, palmata, pedata, scabriuscula, sororia, striata	Violets

SHRUBS, TREES, AND VINES - 1700-1776

Abies balsamea	Balsam
Acacia farnesiana	Egyptian Acacia
Acer negundo	Box Elder
Acer pennsylvanicum	Moosewood, Striped Maple
Acer platanoides	Norway Maple
Acer saccharinum	Silver Maple

Acer saccharum	Sugar Maple
Aesculus hippocastanum	Horse Chestnut, "roasted and eaten to stop the flux"
Aesculus octandra	Sweet Buckeye
Aesculus pavia	Dwarf Horse Chestnut, Red Buckeye
Albizzia julibrissin	Mimosa, Silk Tree
Alnus rugosa	Alder
Amelanchier canadensis	Shadblow, Service Tree or Shad-bush
Amelanchier ovalis	Snowy Mespilus
Amorpha fruticosa	Amorpha, Bastard Indigo, False Indigo
Aralia spinosa	Aralia or Devil's Walking Stick
Aronia arbutifolia	Red Chokeberry
Artemesia abrotanum	Southernwood, Old Man
Asimina triloba	Pawpaw
Baccharis halimifolia	Groundsel Tree
Berberis vulgaris	Barberry
Betula lenta	Black Birch
Betula nigra	River Birch
Bignonia capreolata	Cross-vine
Broussonetia papyrifera	Common Paper Mulberry
Buxus sempervirens arborescens	Tree Box
Buxus sempervirens aurea maculata	Gilded Box
Buxus sempervirens pendula	Weeping Box
Buxus sempervirens suffruticosa	Dwarf Box
Callicarpa americana	Callicarpa, French Mulberry, American Beautyberry
Calycanthus floridus	Carolina Allspice, Sweetshrub or Sweet-scented shrub
Caragana arborescens	Siberian Peashrub
Carpinus caroliniana	American Hornbeam
Carya laciniosa	Shell-bark Hickory
Carya ovata	Scaly-bark Hickory
Carya pecan	Pecan, Mississippi Nut
Castanea pumila	Chinquapin
Catalpa bignonioides	Catalpa, Southern Catalpa
Ceanothus americanus	New Jersey Tea
Celastrus scandens	American Bittersweet, Climbing Staff Tree, Waxwork, False or Shrubby Bittersweet
Cephalanthus occidentalis	Button Bush
Chamaecyparis thyoides	Atlantic White Cedar
Chimonanthus praecox	Wintersweet
Chionanthus virginica	Fringe Tree
Clematis virginiana	Clematis, Virgin's Bower
Clethra alnifolia	Clethra, Sweet Pepper Bush
Comptonia peregrina	Sweet Fern
Cornus alba	White Cornel, White-berried Dogwood, Tartarian Dogwood
Cornus florida rubra	Pink Flowering Dogwood
Coronilla emerus	Emerus

Crataegus crus-galli	Hawthorn, Cock-spur, Haw
Crataegus oxycantha	Hawthorn, English Hawthorn
Crataegus phaenopyrum	Hawthorn, Wahington Thorn
Crataegus punctatus	Large-berried Thorn, Great-fruited Thorn
Cyrilla racemiflora	Swamp Cyrilla
Cytisus scoparius	Scotch Broom
Diospyros virginiana	Persimmon
Dirca palustris	Leatherwood
Elaeagnus angustifolia	Russian Olive - narrow-leaved Oleaster
Euonymus atropurpureus	Burning Bush
Exochorda racemosa	Pearl Bush
Fagus grandifolia	American Beech
Fagus sylvatica	European Beech
Fothergilla gardeni	Dwarf Fothergilla
Franklinia alatamaha	Franklinia - It was grown by John Bartram in his botanical garden but never used extensively in garden plantings.
Fraxinus americana	American or White Ash
Fraxinus excelsior	European Ash
Gleditsia triacanthos	Honey Locust
Gymnocladus dioica	Kentucky Coffee Tree, Kentucky Coffeebean
Halesia carolina	Carolina Silver-bell, Snowdrop Tree
Hedera helix	English Ivy
Hydrangea aborescens	Hydrangea
Hypericum calycinum	St. John's Wort
Ilex aquifolium	Evergreen English Holly
Ilex cassine	Dahoon
Ilex decidua	Swamp Holly, Possumhaw
Ilex glabra	Inkberry
Ilex opaca	Evergreen, American Holly
Ilex verticillata	Winterberry, Swamp Red-berry Bush - Winterberry is mentioned before 1700 and is probably either this plant or I. glabra.
Ilex vomitoria	Cassine, Cassioberry, Yaupon, Cassena
Itea virginica	Virginian Willow, Sweet Spire
Jasminum officinale	White Flowered Jassmine
Juglans cinerea	Butternut
Juniperus chinensis	Chinese Juniper
Juniperus communis	Juniper
Kalmia latifolia	Mountain Laurel, Ivy Laurel
Koelreuteria paniculata	Golden Rain Tree
Lagerstroemia indica	Crape Myrtle
Leucothoe axillaris	Leucothoe
Lonicera tartarica	Tartarian Honeysuckle
Lyonia ligustrina	Andromeda
Maclura pomifera	Osage Orange
Magnolia acuminata	Cucumber Tree
Magnolia grandiflora	Southern Magnolia, Carolina Laurel
Magnolia tripetala	Umbrella Magnolia

94

Malus coronaria	Anchor Tree
Melia azedarach	Chinaberry, Pride of China, Bead Tree
Myrica gale	Bayberry, Sweet Gale
Nyssa sylvatica	Sour Gum, Pepperidge, Black Gum, Tupelo or Black Tupelo
Ostrya virginiana	Ironwood, Hop Tree
Oxydendrum arboreum	Sourwood, Sorrel Tree, Andromeda Tree
Persea borbonia	Redbay or Bull Bay
Persea palustris	Swamp Redbay
Pinus strobus	White Pine
Pinus taeda	Loblolly Pine
Pinus virginiana	Virginia Scrub Pine
Populus deltoides	Eastern Poplar
Potentilla fruticosa	Potentilla
Prunus caroliniana	Cherry Laurel
Prunus cerasifera	Cherry Plum, Myrobalan Plum
Prunus domestica var. institia	Bullace Plum, Damson Plum
Prunus glandulosa	Flowering Almond
Prunus maritima	Beach Plum
Ptelea trifoliata	Trefoil, Hop Tree
Punica granatum var. nana	Bantum Pomegranate
Pyracantha coccinea	Scarlet or Everlasting Firethorn - Pyracantha referred to before 1700 but without scientific name. Probably is this one.
Quercus falcata	Southern Red Oak
Quercus marilandica	Blackjack Oak
Quercus nigra	Water Oak
Quercus phellos	Willow Oak
Quercus prinus	Chestnut Oak
Quercus velutina	Black Oak
Quercus virginiana	Live Oak
Rhododendron calendulaceum	Flame Azalea
Rhododendron indicum	Indica Azalea
Rhododendron nudiflorum	Wild Honeysuckle, Pinxterbloom Azalea Upright American Honeysuckle
Rhododendron viscosum	Swamp White Azalea
Rhus aromatica	Fragrant Sumac
Rhus toxicodendron	Poison Oak
Robinia hispida	Pink Locust, Roseacacia Locust
Rosa laevigata	Cherokee Rose
Rosa palustris	Wild Rose, Swamp Rose
Rosa spinosissima	Scotch Rose
Ruscus aculeatus	Butchersbroom or Prickly Butcher's Broom
Salix alba var. vitellina	Yellow Willow
Salix babylonica	Weeping Willow
Sambucus canadensis	American Elder
Sophora japonica	Japanese Pagoda Tree
Spartium junceum	Spanish Broom

Spirea tomentosa	Spirea or Hardhack
Stewartia malachodendron	Stewartia
Stewartia ovata	Mountain Stewartia
Symphoricarpos orbiculatus	Indian Currant or Indiancurrent, Coralberry
Syringa persica	Persian Lilac or Persian Jasmine
Taxodium distichum	Bald or Deciduous Cypress
Taxus baccata	English Yew
Taxus canadensis	American Yew
Tilia americana	American Linden
Tilia europaea	Linden, or European Lime
Ulmus alata	Winged Elm
Ulmus americana	American Elm
Vaccinium vitis-idaea	Cowberry or Lingon, European Red Huckleberry, Bill-berry
Viburnum acerifolium	Mapleleaf Viburnum
Viburnum cassinoides	Witherod
Viburnum dentatum	Arrowwood
Viburnum lentago	Nanyberry or Sheepberry
Viburnum prunifolium	Black Haw, Blackhaw Viburnum
Vitex agnus-castus	Chaste Tree
Vitis rotundifolia	Muscadine Grape
Wisteria frutescens	American Wisteria

VEGETABLES AND FIELD CROPS - 1700-1776

Apium graveolens var. dulce	Celery
Brassica napa	Rape
Brassica oleracea var. botrytis	Broccoli
Capsicum frutescens var. longum	Cayenne Pepper, Guinea Pepper
Cochlearia officinalis	Scurvy Grass
Dioscorea alata	Yam
Fagopyrum esculentum	Buckwheat
Gossypium herbaceum	Cotton
Hibiscus esculentus	Okra
Indigofera anil	West Indian Indigo
Indigofera tinctoria	Indigo
Lagenaria	Squash, Calabash, Bottle Gourd
Lens esculenta	Lentil
Lepidium sativum	Pepper Grass, Garden Cress
Rumex acetosa	Sorrel
Vicia sp.	Vetch
Vigna sinensis	Black-eyed Pea

FRUITS AND NUTS - 1700-1776

Castanea dentata	Chestnut
Castanea sativa	French Chestnut
Diospyrus virginiana	Persimmon
Juglans regia	English Walnut
Juglans nigra	Black Walnut

Malus angustifolia	Crab Apple
Morus alba	White Mulberry
Morus nigra	English Mulberry, Blackberry Tree
Morus rubra	Red or American Mulberry
Olea europaea	Olive
Ribis nigrum	European Black Currant
Rubus sp.	Blackberry - collected from the wild but not cultivated.
Vaccinium macrocarpum	Cranberry - gathered but not cultivated.

ANNUALS AND PERENNIALS - 1776-1850

Achillea ptarmica, flora-plen	Double Sneezewort
Aconitum lycoctonum	Great Yellow Monk's Hood, Wolfsbane
Aconitum napellus, var. album	White Monk's Hood
Aconitum uncinatum	American Monk's Hood, Wolfsbane
Actea spicata	Herb Christopher, White Snakeroot, Black Baneberry
Adlumia fungosa	Spongy-flowered Fumitory, Climbing Fumitory, Mountain Fringe, Allegheny-vine
Adonis aestivalis	Tall Adonis, Summer Adonis
Adonis autumnalis	Flos Adonis, Bird's Eye, Pheasant's-eye
Adonis vernalis	Perennial Adonis, Pheasants-eye, Spring Adonis
Adoxa moshatellina	Tuberous Moschatel, Musk-root
Agnostemma githago	Corn Rose Campion, Corn Cockle
Allionia sp.	Glacous Allionia
Allium moly	Yellow Garlick, Molly
Allium oleraceum	Purple-striped Garlick
Allium ramosum or tuberosum	Sweet-scented Garlick
Allium roseum	Rose Garlick
Alyssum halimifolium	Sweet Alyssum
Amaranthus hybridus,var. hypochondriacus	Blue Amethyst, Prince's Feather
Amethystea caerulea	Blue Amethyst
Anagallis arvensis	Red Pimpernel, Poor Man's Weatherglass
Anarrhinum bellidifolium	Daisy-leaved Toad-flax
Anemone hortensis	Garden Anemone
Anemonella thalictroides	Rue-anemone
Apocynum androsaemifolium	Tutsan-leaved Dog's-bane, Spreading Dog-bane
Aquilegia alpina	Alpine Columbine
Aquilegia vulgaris	European Columbine
Arctotis sp.	Chamomile Arctotis
Arethusa bulbosa	Bulbous Arethusa
Argemone mexicana	Prickley Argemone
Arisaema triphyllum	Indian Turnep, Three-leaved Arum, Jack-in-the-pulpit
Armeria maritima var. elongata	Sea Pink, Statice Armeria
Armeria plantaginea	Plantain-leaved Thrift

Aruncus sylvester	Goat's-beard Spiraea
Asclepias incarnata	Flesh-colored Swallow-Wort, Swamp Milkweed
Asclepias purpurascens	Purple Virginian Swallow-wort
Asclepias rubra	Red Swallow-wort
Asclepias syriaca	Syrian Swallow-wort
Asclepias tuberosa, probably	Pleuresy-root, Butterfly-weed
Asclepias verticillata	Verticillate Swallow-wort, Horsetail Milkweed
Asphodelus ramosus	Branched Asphodel
Aster alpinus	Alpine Starwort, "above 50 other sp."
Aster grandiflorus	Catesby's Starwort
Aster novae-angliae	New England Starwort, New England Aster
Aster undulatus	Waved Starwort
Astragalus galegiformis	Goat's rue-leaved Astragalus
Aureolaria flava	Yellow-flowered Gerardia
Aureolaria pedicularia	Louse-wort-leaved Gerardia
Baptisia alba	White Podalyria or White False or Wild Indigo
Baptisia australis	Blue or Sophora Podalyria or False or Wild Indigo
Baptisia tinctoria	Yellow Podalyria or Bastard Indigo
Browallia americana	Upright Browallia, blue & white
Bupleurum rotundifolia	Round-leaved Hare's ear or Thorough-wax
Bupthalmum grandiflorum	Great-flowered Ox-eye
Calceolaria pinnata	Pinnated Slipper-wort
Calonyction aculeatum	Prickly Ipomoea or Common Moonflower
Calopogon pulchellus	Tuberous-rooted Limodorum or Grass-pink Orchid
Caltha palustris var. monstrosa-pleno	Double Marsh Marigold
Campanula carpatica	Heart-leaved Bell-flower, Tussock Bell-flower
Campanula glomerata	Clustered Bell-flower
Campanula persicifolia var. grandiflora	Great-flowered Bell-flower
Campanula pyramidalis	Pyramidal Bell-flower, Chimney Bellflower
Campanula rapunculoides	Nettle-leaved Bell-flower, Rover Bell-flower
Campanula trachelium	Great Bell-flower
Cardamine pratensis	Double Ladies-smock or Cuckoo-flower
Cardiospermum halicacabum	Smooth-leaved Heart-seed, Balloon-vine
Carpanthea pomeridiana	Great Yellow-flowered Fig Marigold
Carthamus tinctorius	Bastard Saffron, Safflower, False Saffron
Cassia fasciculata	Dwarf Cassia, Partridge Pea
Cassia marilandica	Maryland Cassia, Wild Senna
Catananche caerulea	Blue Catananche
Celsia orientalis	Oriental Celsia
Centaurea alpina	Alpine Centaury
Centaurea glastifolia	Woad-leaved Centaury
Centaurea montana	Mountain Blue-bottle, Mountain Bluet
Centaurea moschata	Sweet Purple Sultan, Sweet Sultan

Centaurea moschata var. alba	White Sweet Sultan
Centaurium sp.	American Centaury
Centranthus ruber	Red Garden Valerian, Jupiter's Beard
Cerinthe major	Great Purple Honey-Wort
Chelone obliqua	Red Chelone
Chenopodium botrys	Sweet-scented Goosefoot, Feather Geranium or Jerusalem Oak
Chenopodium capitatum	Berry-headed Blite
Chrysanthemum carinatum	Three-coloured Chrysanthemum
Chrysanthemum coronarium	Garden Chrysanthemum, Garland Chrysanthemum or Crown Daisy
Chrysanthemum indicum	Indian Chrysanthemum
Chrysoplenium alternafolium	Alternate-leaved Golden Saxifrage
Cimicifuga racemosa	Black Snake Root
Claytonia virginica	Virginian Claytonia
Clematis integrifolia	Entire-leaved Virgin's Bower
Clematis ochroleuca	Yellow-flowered Virgin's Bower
Clematis recta	Upright Virgin's Bower
Cleome sp.	Five-leaved Cleome
Cleome sp.	Violet-coloured Cleome
Coix lacryma-jobi	Job's Tears
Convolvulus tricolor	Minor Convalvulus, Dwarf Morning Glory
Coreopsis auriculata	Ear-leaved Coreopsis
Coreopsis verticillata	Whorl-leaved Coreopsis, Thread-leaf Coreopsis
Coronilla varia	Purple Coronilla, Crown Vetch
Corydalis capnoides (probably)	White-flowered Fumitory
Corydalis cava	Hollow Rooted Fumitory
Corydalis cava, var. bulbosa	Bulbous Fumitory
Corydalis lutea (probably)	Yellow Fumitory
Corydalis sempervirens	Glaucous Fumitory, Roman Wormwood
Crepis rubra	Red Hawkweed or Hawks Beard
Crocus susianus	Crocus or Cloth of Gold
Cryophytum nodiflorum	Egyptian Fig Marigold
Cryptostemma calendulaceum	Marigold-flowered Arctotis
Cucumis melo var. flexuosus	Snake or Melon Cucumber, "grown as a curiosity"
Cucumis melo var. dudaim	Dudaim Cucumber, "highly perfumed"
Cucurbita pepo var. ovifera	Egg Gourd, "many forms & colors of small hard-shelled ornamental durable fruits"
Cypripedium acaule	Two-leaved Purple Lady's Slipper, Pink Lady's Slipper
Cypripedium calceolus	English Lady's Slipper, Yellow Lady-slipper of Eurasia
Datura metel	Double Purple Stramonium
Delphinium elatum	Bee Larkspur
Delphinium elatum, var. intermedium	Palmated Bee Larkspur
Delphinium exaltatum	American Larkspur
Dianthus carthusianorum	Carthusian Pink, Clusterhead Pink

99

Dianthus chinensis	China Pink, Rainbow Pink
Dianthus deltoides	Maiden or Common Pink
Dianthus superbus	Superb Pink
Dicentra cucullaria	Naked-stalked Fumitory or Dutchman's Breeches
Dictamnus albus var. rubra	Red-flowered Fraxinella, Dittany, Gasplant, Burning Bush
Digitalis ferruginea	Iron-coloured Fox-glove, Rusty Fox-glove
Digitalis lutea	Small Yellow Fox-glove, Straw Foxglove
Digitalis purpurea var. alba	White-flowered Fox-glove
Dimorphotheca annua	Small Cape Marigold
Dimorphotheca hybrida	Large Cape Marigold
Dodecatheon meadia	American Cowslip, Shooting Star
Dolichus lablab	Black-seeded Dolichus, Hyacinth Bean, Bonavist, Lablab
Dracocephalum austriacum	Austrian Dragon's Head
Dracocephalum grandiflorum	Great-flowered Dragon's Head
Dracocephalum moldavica	Moldavian Balm
Dracocephalum nutans	Nodding Dragon's Head
Dracocephalum thymiflorum	Thyme-leaved Dragon's Head
Ecballium elaterium	Squirting Cucumber
Echinacea angustifolia	Narrow-leaved Rudbeckia
Echinacea purpurea	Purple Rudbeckia, Purple Coneflower
Echinops ritro	Small Globe Thistle
Echinops sphaerocephalus	Great Globe Thistle
Emilia sagittata	Scarlet-flowered Cacalia, Tassel Flower, Flora's Paintbrush
Epilobium angustifolium	Narrow-leaved Willow-herb, Fireweed, Giant Willow-herb
Eryngium alpinum	Alpine Eryngium
Erythronium americanum	American Erythronium
Eupatorium altissimum	Tall Eupatorium
Eupatorium coelestinum	Blue-flowered Eupatorium, Mist Flower, "there are many others"
Euphorbia lathyrus	Caper Spurge, Mole Plant, "there are many others"
Euphorbia marginata	Snow-on-the-mountain
*Filipendula hexapetala**	*Filipendula or Dropwort*
Filipendula ulmaria	Meadow Sweet, Queen-of-the-meadow
Fritillaria camschatcensis	Kamptschatka Lily
Fritillaria pyrenaica	Black Fritillary
Galega officinalis	Goat's-rue or Officinal Galega
Gaura sp.	Biennial Gaura
Gentiana acaulis	Dwarf Gentian or Gentianella, Stemless Gentian
Gentiana crinita	Fringed-flowered Gentian, Fringed Gentian
Gentiana lutea	Yellow Gentian
Gentiana purpurea	Purple Gentian
Gentiana saponaria	Soap-wort-leaved Gentian

100

Gentiana villosa	Hoary Gentian
Geranium aconitifolium	Aconite-leaved Geranium
Geranium macrorrhizum	Large-rooted Crane's-bill
Geranium striatum	Streaked Geranium
Gladiolus communis	European Corn-flag*
Gladiolus segetum	Round-seeded Corn-flag, Cornflag
Glaucium flavum	Yellow Horned Poppy, Sea Poppy
Globularia cordifolia	Cordate-leaved Globularia
Globularia vulgaris	European Globularia or Blue Daisy
Hedysarum coronarium	French Honeysuckle
Helenium autumnale	Smooth Helenium, Sneezeweed
Helianthus annuus var. nanus	Dwarf Annual Sunflower
Helianthus atrorubens	Dark Red Sunflower, Dark-eye Sunflower
Helianthus decapetalus	Many-flowered Perennial Sunflower, Thinleaf Sunflower
Helianthus giganteus	Gigantic Sunflower
Helleborus foetidus	Stinking Bear's-foot
Helleborus probably orientalis	Livid or Purple Hellebore
Helleborus viridis	Green Hellebore
Helonias bullata	Spear-leaved Helonias, Swamp Pink
Hepatica americana or nobilis	Common Hepatica, Liverleaf
Hermodactylus tuberosus	Snakes-head Iris
Hesperis tristis	Night Smiling Rocket
Heuchera americana	American Heuchera or Sanicle, Alum Root
Hibiscus speciosus	Specious Smooth Hibiscus
Hibiscus militaris	Halbert-leaved Hibiscus, Soldier Rose Mallow
Hibiscus trionum	Bladder Hibiscus or Ketmia, Flower-of-an-hour
Hippocrepis multisiliquosa	Many-podded or Horseshoe Vetch
Houstonia caerulea	Blue Flowered Houstonia, Bluets
Houstonia purpurea	Purple-flowered Houstonia
Hyacinthus amethystinus	Amethyst-coloured Hyacinth
Hyacinthus romanus	Roman Grape Hyacinth
Hydrastis canadensis	Canadian Yellow-root, Goldenseal or Orange Root
*Hypericum calycinum**	Large-flowered St. John's-wort
Hypericum hirsutum	Hairy St. John's-wort
Hypoxis hirsuta	Upright Hypoxis
Iberis amara	White Candy-tuft, Rocket Candy-tuft
Iberis odorata	Sweet-scented Candy-tuft
Iberis umbellata	Purple Candy-tuft, Globe Candy-tuft - First species introduced. Brought from Candia, thus the name.
Impatiens noli-tangere	Touch Me Not
Ipomoea purpurea	Common Morning Glory
Iris fulva	
Iris pumila	Iris, Dwarf Flag
Iris sibirica	Siberian Iris
Iris sisyrinchium	Crocus-rooted Iris

Iris versicolor	Various-colored Iris
Iris virginica	Virginian Iris
Iris xiphium	Iris, Spanish Flag or Bulbous Iris
Ixia chinensis	Chinese Ixia
Jeffersonia diphylla	Binate-leaved Jeffersonia, Twin-leaf
Kickxia elatine	Fluellin or Toad-flax
Kochia scoparia	Belvedere, Summer Cypress
Lathyrus sativus	Blue Chickling Vetch, Grass Pea
Lathyrus tingitanus	Tangier Pea
Lavatera thuringiaca	Great-flowered Lavatera
Lavatera trimestris	European Lavatera
Leucojum aestivum	Summer Snowdrop
Leucojum autumnale	Autumnal Snowdrop
Liatris elegans (probably)	Hairy-cupped Liatris - Liatris is also known as Blazing Star, Gay-feather, or Button Snakeroot.
Liatris pilosa	Hairy-leaved Liatris
Liatris spicata	Long-spiked Liatris
Lilium candidum	Common White Lily, Madonna Lily
Lilium catesbaei	Catesby's Lily, Southern Red Lily
Lilium croceum	Bulb-bearing or Orange Lily
Lilium philadelphicum	Philadelphia Lily, Orangecup Lily, Wood Lily
Lilium pomponium	Pomponean Lily
Lilium speciosum	Speciosum Lily
Lilium superbum	Superb Lily, American Turks Cap Lily
Linaria purpurea	Purple Toad-flax
Linum perenne	Perennial Flax
Lobularia maritima (probably)	Sweet Alyssum
Lobelia siphilitica	Blue Cardinal's Flower
Lopezia coronata	Mexican Lopezia
Lotus tetragonolobus	Winged Pea
Lupinus albus	White Annual Lupin
Lupinus angustifolius	Narrow-leaved Blue Lupin
Lupinus hirsutus	Great Blue Lupin
Lupinus luteus	Yellow Lupin
Lupinus pilosus	Rose Lupin
Lupinus varius	Small Blue Lupin
Lupinus perennis	Perennial Lupin, Sun Dial Lupin
Lychnis coeli-rosa	Smooth-leaved Rose Campion, Rose-of-heaven
Lychnis flos-cuculi	Meadow Lychnis, Cuckoo Flower or Ragged Robin
Lychnis flos-jovis	Umbelled Campion, Flower of Jove
Lysimachia quadrifolia	Four-leaved Loose-strife
Lythrum salicaria	Purple European Willow-herb, Purple Loosestrife
Lythrum virgatum	Fine-leaved Willow-herb
Malcomia maritima	Annual Stock or Mediterranean Stock
Malva crispa	Curled Mallow
Medicago intertexta	Medic, Hedgehog

Medicago scutellata	Medic, Snail, Snails
Melanthium latifolium	Spear-leaved Melanthium
Melanthium virginicum	Virginian Melanthium, Bunch Flower
Menyanthes trifoliata	English Buck-bean, also Bog Bean
Mimulus alatus	Wing-stalked Monkey-flower
Mimulus ringens	Oblong-leaved Monkey-flower
Mirabilis dichotomo	Forked Marvel of Peru, Marvel of Peru, Four O'Clock
Mirabilis longiflora	Sweet-scented Marvel of Peru
Mirabilis viscosa	Clammy Marvel of Peru
Molucella laevis	Smooth Molucca Balm, Shell Flower
Molucella spinosa	Prickly Molucca Balm
Momordica Balsamina	Male Balsam Apple
Momordica charantia	Hairy Balsam Apple or Balsam Pear
Monarda punctata	Yellow-flowered Monarda or Horse Mint
Muscari racemosum	Clustered Grape Hyacinth
Narcissus biflorus	Two-flowered Narcissus, Primrose Peerless Narcissus
Narcissus bulbocodium	Hoop-petticoat Narcissus, Petticoat Daffodil
Narcissus moschatus	Musk-scented Narcissus
Narcissus odorus	Sweet-scented Narcissus, Campernelle Jonquil
Narcissus pseudo-narcissus	Common Daffodil, Trumpet Narcissus
N. psuedo narcissus, form bicolor	Two-coloured Narcissus
N. tazetta, form. bicolor	Two-coloured Narcissus
N. minor, form bicolor	Small Narcissus
Narcissus serotinus	Late-flowering Narcissus
Narcissus tazetta	Polyanthus Narcissus
Narcissus tazetta var. orientalis	Oriental Narcissus, Chinese Sacred Lily
Narcissus triandrus	Rush-leaved Narcissus
Nelumbium pentapetalum	Yellow Indian Water Lily, American Lotus, Water Chinkapin
Nigella hispanica	Fenel-flower, Devil in a Bush
Nolana prostrata	Trailing Nolana
Nuphae advenum	Three-coloured Water Lily
Nuphae luteum	Yellow Water Lily
Nymphaea alba	European White Water Lily
Nymphaea odorata	American Sweet-scented White Water Lily
Oenothera fruticosa	Shrubby Primrose-tree
Oenothera perennis	Dwarf Primrose-tree
Oenothera tetraptera	Changeable Primrose-tree
Ophrys apifera	Bee Ophrys
Orchis spectabilis	Shewy Orchis, Showy Orchis
Ornithogalum pyramidale	Pyramidal Star of Bethlehem
Ornithogalum thyrsoides	Yellow Star of Bethlehem
Ornithogalum umbellatum	Umbelled Star of Bethlehem

Oxalis violacea	Purple Oxalis, Wood Sorrel
Oxybaphus sp.	Viscid Umbrella-wort
Paeonia albiflora	White-flowered Peony
Paeonia anomala or a var.	
of Paeonia tenuifolia	Jagged-leaved Peony
Paeonia tenuifolia	Slender-leaved Peony
Pancratium maritimum	Sea Pancratium
Papaver dubium	Smooth Poppy
Papaver rhoeas	Corn Poppy
Papaver somniferum	Common White Poppy, also double-flowered in all sorts
Paradisea liliastrum	St. Bruno's Lily
Passiflora lutea	Yellow Passion-flower
Penstemom hirsutus	Hairy Penstemon
Penstemon laevigatus	Smooth Penstemon
Phaseolus coccineus	Scarlet-flowering Kidney Bean
Phlox carolina	Carolina Phlox, Lychnadea, Thick-leaf Phlox
Phlox drummondii	Annual or Drummond Phlox
Phlox nivalis	Fine-leaved Phlox, Trailing Phlox
Phlox ovata	Oval-leaved Phlox
Phlox pilosa	Hairy Phlox
Phlox stolonifera	Creeping or Daisy-leaved Phlox
Phlox subulata	Awl-shaped Phlox, Ground or Moss Pink
Physostegia virginiana	Virginian Dragon's Head, False Dragonhead
Podophyllum peltatum	May Apple
Polemonium caeruleum	Blue European Valerian, Jacob's Ladder, Greek Valerian, Charity
Polemonium caeruleum var.	
album	White Valerian
Polemonium reptans	Creeping Greek Valerian
Polygala lutea	Yellow Annual Milkwort
Polygala senega	Officinal Milkwort, Seneca Snakeroot or Rattle-snake Root
Polyganatum multiflorum	Many-flowered Solomon's-seal
Polygonum orientale	Tall Persicaria, Princes Feather
Polygonum persicaria	Persicaria, Ladys Thumb
Pontederia cordata	Heart-leaved Pontederia, Pickerel-weed
Potentilla grandiflora	Great-flowered Potentilla
Primula elatior	Oxslip or Polyanthus
Primula farinosa	Bird's-eye Cowslip
Primula glutinosa	Clammy Primrose
Primula longifolia	Long-leaved Primrose
Primula marginata	Silver-edged Primrose
Primula polyantha, forma	
Hose-in-Hose	Hose-in-Hose Primrose
Primula veris	Cowslip
Proboscidea sp.	Unicorn Plant or Cuckold's Horns
Prunella grandiflora	Great-flowered Self-heal

Pyrola rotundifolia	Round-leaved Winter-green
Quamoclit coccinea	Scarlet Ipomoea, Star Ipomoea
Quamoclit coccinea var.	
hederifolia	Ivy-leaved Ipomoea
Quamoclit pennata	Cypress Vine, Winged-leaved Ipomoea
Ranunculus aconitifolius	Fair Maids of France
Ranunculus acris, flo. pleno	Double Upright Crowfoot
Ranunculus bulbosus, flore-pleno	Double Bulbous Crowsfoot
Ranunculus ficaria	Pilewort (double & single)
Ranunculus gramineus	Grass-leaved Crowfoot
Reseda odorata	Mignonette
Rhexia mariana	Maryland Rhexia
Rhexia virginica	Hairy-leaved Rhexia
Ricinus communis	Castor-oil Plant or Palma Christi
Rudbeckia fulgida	Bright Rudbeckia
Rudbeckia laciniata	Jagged-leaved Rudbeckia
Rumex patientia	Dock, Patience
Salvia hispanica	Spanish Sage
Salvia lyrata	Lyre-leaved Sage
Saponaria ocymoides	Basil-leaved Soapwort
Sarracenia flava	Yellow Side-saddle Flower, Pitcher Plant
Sarracenia minor	Small Side-saddle Flower
Sarracenia purpurea	Purple Side Saddle Flower
Sarracenia rubra	Red Side Saddle Flower
Saxifraga cotyledon	Pyramidal Saxifrage
Saxifraga granulata	White Granulous-rooted Saxifrage, Meadow Saxifrage
Saxifraga hypnoides	Mossy Saxifrage or Lady's Cushion
Saxifraga sarmentosa	Strawberry Saxifrage, Strawberry Geranium
Saxifraga umbrosa	London Pride
Saxifraga virginiensis	Virginian Saxifrage
Scilla autumnalis	Squill
Scilla bifolia	Two-leaved Squill
Scilla italica	Italian Squill
Scilla peruviana	Squill
Scorpiurus muricata	Two-flowered Caterpillar
Scorpiurus sulcata	Furrowed Caterpillar
Scorpiurus vermiculata	One-flowered Caterpillar
Scutellaria integrifolia	Entire-leaved Scul-cap, Skullcap
Sedum aizoon	Yellow Stonecrop, Live-for-ever, also a common name for Sedums
Sedum album	White Stonecrop
Sedum anacamperseros	Evergreen Orpine
Sempervivum arachnoideum	Cobweb Houseleek
Sempervivum montanum	Mountain Houseleek
Sempervivum montanum, form globiferum	Globular Houseleek

Senecio elegans	Elegant Groundsel, Purple Jacoboea, Purple Ragwort
Sesamum orientale	Oriental Sesamum, Oily-grain, Sesame
Silene alpestris	Austrian Catchfly, Alpine Catchfly
Silene armeria	Lobel's Catchfly, Sweet William Catchfly
Siline caroliniana	Pennsylvanian Catchfly, Wild Pink
Silene pendula	Pendulous Catchfly
Silene virginica	Virginian Catchfly, Fire Pink
Silphium laciniatum	Jagged-leaved Silphium, Compass Plant, Silphiums are also known as Rosinweed
Silphium perfoliatum	Square-stalked Silphium, Cup Plant, Indian Cup
Silphium terebinthinum	Broad-leaved Silphium, Prairie Dock
Silphium trifoliatum	Three-leaved Silphium
Sisyrinchium bermudiana	Bermudian Sisyrinchium - The plants of this genus are also known as Blue-eyed-grass
Sisyrinchium graminoides	Grass-leaved Sisyrinchium
Sisyrinchium mucronatum	Pointed Sisyrinchium
Soldanella alpina	Alpine Soldanella
Solidago altissima	Tall Golden-rod
Solidago flexicaulis	Figwort-leaved Golden-rod
Solidago graminifolia	Lance-leaved Golden-rod
Solidago latifolia	Broad-leaved Golden-rod
Solidago odora	Sweet-scented Golden-rod
Smilacina racemosa (probably)	Cluster-flowered Solomon's-seal
Specularia speculum-veneris	Venus Looking Glass
Spigelia marilandica	Carolina Pink-root
Stachys grandiflora	Great-flowered Betony - Plants of this genus are also known as Woundworts
Stachys lanata	Wooly Stachys, Lambs Ears
Teucrium flavum	Tree Germander
Thalictrum dioicum	Dioecious Meadow-rue
Thalictrum polygamum	Meadow-rue
Tolpis barbata	Yellow Hawkweed, Golden Yellow Hawkweed
Tradescantia virginiana	Virginian Spider-wort, Common Spiderwort
Trifolium incarnatum	Crimson-spiked Clover
Trillium cernum	Nodding-flowered Trillium
Trillium erectum	Erect-flowered Trillium
Trillium pusillum	Dwarf Trillium
Trillium sessile	Sessile-flowered Trillium
Trillium undulatum	Red-fruited Trillium
Triosteum perfoliatum	Fever Root, Horse Gentian or Feverwort
Tulipa sylvestris	Italian Yellow Tulip
Urtica pilulifera	Roman Nettle
Vallisneria americana	American Vallisneria
Vallisneria spiralis	European Vallisneria, Eel Grass or Tape Grass
Veratrum viride	Green-flowered Veratrum
Verbascum blattaria	Moth Mullein
Verbascum phoeniceum	Purple Mullein

Verbesina encelioides	Annual Xeminesia
Veronicastrum virginicum	Virginian Speedwell, Culvers Root
Vicia oroboides	Upright Bitter Vetch
Vigna sesquipedalis	Long-podded Dolichos or Asparagus Bean, Yard Long Bean
Viola lanceolata	Lance-leaved Violet
Viola odorata, flo-plen	Double Sweet-scented Violet, Sweet Garden or Florists Violet
Viola primulifolia	Primrose-leaved Violet
Viola pubescens	Downey Violet
Viola rotundifolia	Yellow Round-leaved Violet
Xeranthemum annuum	Eternal Flower, Common Immortelle
Zephyranthes atamasco	Atamasco Lily
Zinnia elegans	Violet-coloured Zinnia, Youth-and-old-age
Zinnia multiflora	Red Zinnia
Zinnia panciflora	Yellow Zinnia

SHRUBS, TREES & VINES - 1776-1850

Abies alba	Silver Fir
Acer palmatum	Japanese Maple
*Acer platinoides**	Norway Maple
Acer pseudo-platanus	European Sycamore, Sycamore Maple
Acer spicatum	Mountain Maple
*Acer saccharinum**	Silver Maple
Aesculus flava	Yellow-flowering Horse Chestnut
*Aesculus hippocastanum**	Horse Chestnut
Ailanthus altissima	Tree-of-heaven
Akebia quinata	Five-leaf Akebia - not in the trade until after 1845
Albizzia julibrissin.*	Silk Tree, Mimosa
Amygdalus persica, florepleno	Double-flowering Peach
Aristolochia durior	Dutchmans Pipe
Berberis canadensis	Canadian Berberry, Allegheny Barberry
Betula lutea	Yellow Birch or Tall Birch
Betula nana	European Dwarf Birch
Betula papyrifera	Canoe or Paper Birch
Betula pendula probably var. tristis or gracilis	Drooping Birch
Betula pendula	Common European or European White Birch
Betula populifolia	Poplar-leaved or Gray Birch
Betula pumila	American Hairy Dwarf Birch
Buxus sempervirens angustifolia	Narrow-leaved Box
Calycanthus fertilis var. ferax	Pennsylvania Sweet Shrub
*Calycanthus floridus**	Carolina Allspice, Sweetshrub, Sweet-scented Shrub
Camellia japonica	Common Camellia - The fashionable specialty of the wealthy in the early 1900's
Carpinus betulus	Common European Hornbeam

107

Carya glabra	Pignut
*Castanea pumila**	Chinquapin
Cedrus atlantica	Atlas Cedar
Cedrus libani	Cedar of Lebanon
*Celtis occidentalis**	American Nettle-tree
Celtis australis	European Nettle-tree
Cercis siliquastrum	European Red-bud
Chaenomeles lagenaria	Flowering Quince
Chamaedaphne calyculata	Globe-flowered Andromeda, Leather Leaf
Cladrastis lutea	Yellow Wood
Clematis cirrhosa	Evergreen Virgin's Bower
Clematis crispa	Curled Virgin's Bower
Clematis orientalis	Oriental Virgin's Bower
Clematis viorna	Leathery-flowered Virgin's Bower
Clematis vitalba	English Virgin's Bower, Traveler's Joy, Old Man's Beard
*Clethra alnifolia**	Sweet Pepperbush or Summer Sweet
Clethra alnifolia var. paniculata	
Colutea arborescens	Bladder Sena
Colutea orientalis	Oriental Sena
Coriaria myrtifolia	Myrtle-leaved Sumach
*Cornus alba**	Tartarian Dogwood
Cornus alternifolia	Alternate-leaved Dogwood
Cornus foemina	Upright Dogwood
Cornus mas	Cornelian Cherry
Cornus racemosa	Panicled Dogwood
Cornus rugosa	Pennsylvania Dogwood
Cornus sanguinea	Red-twigged Dogwood, Bloodtwig Dogwood
Cotoneaster microphylla	Small-leaved Cotoneaster
Crataegus azarolus	Parsley-leaved Azarole
Crataegus viridis	Green-leaved Virginian Hawthorn
Cynara cardunculus	Spanish Cardoon
Cyrilla racemiflora	Swamp Cyrilla
Cytissus sessilifolius	Sessile-leaved Cytissus
Daphne alpina	Alpine Daphne
Daphne cneorum	Trailing Daphne
Daphne laureola	Evergreen Spurge Laurel
Diospyros lotus	European Date Plum
*Elaeagnus angustifolia**	Narrow-leaved Oleaster, Russian Olive
Elaeagnus angustifolia var. spinosa	Thorny Oleaster
Eleagnus umbellatus	Autumn Eleagnus
Euonymus americanus	Evergreen Spindle-tree, Burning Bush
Euonymus europaeus	European Spindle tree
Euonymus japonicus	Evergreen Euonymus
Euonymus latifolius	Broad-leaved Spindletree
Euonymus verrucosus	Warted Spindle tree
Forsythia suspensa sieboldii	Siebold Weeping Forsythia

Fothergilla gardeni *	Dwarf Fothergilla
Franklinia alatamaha *	Franklinia
Fraxinus caroliniana	Red Ash, Water Ash
Fraxinus probably excelsior	
var. pendula	Drooping Ash
Fraxinus nigra	Black American Ash
Fraxinus ornus	True Manna, Flowering Manna, Flowering Ash
Fraxinus rotundifolia	Round-leaved Manna
Gaultheria procumbens	Mountain Tea, Teaberry, Wintergreen, Checkerberry, Tea-berry
Ginko biloba	Maidenhair Tree
Gleditsia aquatica	One-seeded Locust, Water or Swamp Locust
Gleditsia japonica	Long-spined Locust
Gleditsia triacanthos var. inermis	Thornless Locust
Halesia carolina *	Carolina Silver-bell or Snowdrop Tree
Halesia diptera	Two-winged Snowdrop Tree
Hibiscus syriacus	Rose-of-Sharon
Hippophae rhaminoides	Sea Buckthorn
Hydrangea arborescens *	Hydrangea
Hydrangea paniculata	
Hydrangea radiata	Downy Hydrangea
Hypericum kalmianum	Kalmia-leaved St. John's-wort
Ilex aquifolium var. ferox	Hedge-hog Holly - "numerous other varieties, striped, blotched, etc."
Ilex aquifolium var. heterophylla	Various-leaved Holly
Ilex aquifolium var. recurva	Slender-leaved Holly
Ilex cassine *	Dahoon
Ilex laevigata	Smooth Winterberry
Itea cyrilla	Entire Leaved Itea
Jasminum fruticans	Common Yellow Jasmine
Juniperus communis var. suecia	Swedish Juniper
Kalmia angustifolia	Narrow-leaved Kalmia or Laurel, Lambkill, Sheep Laurel
Kalmia polifolia	Glaucus-leaved Kalmia, Bog Kalmia
Kerria japonica florepleno	Crocus Rose
Koelreuteria paniculata *	Golden Rain Tree
Ledum graenlandicum	Broad-leaved Ledum, Labrador Tea
Ledum palustre	Marsh Ledum, Crystal Tea, Wild Rosemary
Leucothoe axillaris *	Leucothoe
Leucothoe racemosa	Branching Andromeda, Sweetbells
Lonicera caprifolium	Italian Honeysuckle
Lonicera japonica	Japanese Honeysuckle
Lyonia mariana	Maryland Andromeda, Stagger Bush
Magnolia acuminata *	Cucumber Tree
Magnolia fraseri	Ear-leaved Magnolia
Magnolia glauca	Glaucus or Swamp Magnolia, Sweet Bay

Magnolia grandiflora var.	
lanceolata	Exmouth Magnolia
Magnolia macrophylla	Big-leaf Magnolia
Magnolia X soulangeana	Saucer Magnolia
Magnolia tripetala	Umbrella Magnolia
Mahonia aquifolium	Oregon Holly-grape
Malus angustifolia	Narrow-leaved Crab, Southern Crabapple
Malus prunifolia	Siberian Crab .
Malus spectabilis	Chinese Apple Tree
Melia azedarach*	Chinaberry, Pride of China, Bead Tree
Menispermum canadense	Canadian Moonseed
Morus alba	White Italian Mulberry
Morus multicaulis	Mulberry - During the era of the "silk mania", 1826-1841, more of these trees were probably sold than any other.
Morus nigra	Black Mulberry
Morus rubra	Red Mulberry or American Mulberry
Myricaria germanica	German Tamarisk, False Tamarisk
Ocimum minimum	Bush Basil - According to Bailey probably a small form of O. Basilicum which appears before 1700.
Ononis fruticosa	Shrubby Rest Harrow
Paeonia suffruticosa	Tree Peony
Paulownia tomentosa	Empress-tree - Not introduced until 1834. It is in trade at least by 1844.
Periploca graeca*	Virginian Silk Tree - Periploca is referred to in 1600's, but without scientific name.
Phillyrea angustifolia	Phillyrea
Phillyrea latifolia	
Phillyrea latifolia var.	
media	
Physocarpus opulifolius	Nine-bark
Picea abies	Fir, Norway Spruce
Picea glauca	Fir, White Spruce
Picea mariana	Fir or Black Spruce
Picea orientalis	Oriental Spruce
Pieris floribunda	Mountain Andromeda
Pinus cembra	Siberian Stone Pine, Swiss Stone Pine
Pinus flexilis	Limber Pine
Pinus mugo	Mugho Pine or Mountain Pine
Pinus pinaster	Cluster Pine, Pinaster
Pinus pinea	Stone Pine, Italian Stone Pine
Pinus resinosa	Pitch Pine - P. resinosa is Red Pine & Pitch Pine is P. rigida according to Bailey
Pinus sylvestris	Scotch Pine
Platanus orientalis*	Oriental Plane Tree
Polygala chamaebuxus	Box-leaved Milkwort
Populus alba	White Poplar

Populus angulata	probably a hybrid between P. balsamifera and P. nigra.
Populus candicans	Balm of Gilead
Populus heterophylla	Swamp Cottonwood, Various Leaved Poplar
Populus nigra	Black Poplar
Populus tremula	European Aspen
Populus tremuloides	Quaking Aspen
Populus nigra var. italica	Lombardy Poplar
Prunus angustifolia	Narrow-leaved Cherry, Chicksaw Plum
Prunus glandulosa	Dwarf-flowering Almond
Prunus lusitanica	Portugal Laurel
Prunus mahaleb	Perfumed Cherry, St. Lucie Cherry
Prunus padus	European Bird Cherry
Prunus pumila	Dwarf Canadian, Sand Cherry
Prunus serrulata	Japanese Flowering Cherry
Prunus spinosa	Blackthorn or Sloe
Pseudotsuga menziesii	Douglas Fir
*Pyracantha coccinea**	Scarlet or Everlasting Firethorn
Pyrus salicifolia	Willow-leaved Crab
*Quercus sp.**	Oak - McMahon now lists 29 species including some already mentioned in 1700's.
Rhamnus catharticus	Purging Buckthorn
Rhamnus frangula	Berry-bearing Alder
Rhododendron camtschaticum	Rhododendron Kamptschatka
Rhododendron canadense	Canada Rhodora
Rhododendron catawbiense	Catawba Rhododendron
Rhododendron caucasicum	Mt. Caucasus Rhododendron
Rhododendron chrysanthum	Dwarf Rhododendron
Rhododendron dauricum	Dotted-leaved Rhododendron
Rhododendron ferrugineum	Rusty-leaved Rhododendron
Rhododendron hirsutum	Hairy Rhododendron
Rhododendron indicum	Indian Azalea
Rhododendron maximum	Rhododendron or Broad-leaved Mountain Laurel
Rhodothamnus chamaecistus	Austrian Rhododendron
Rhus copallina	Lentiscus-leaved Sumac
Rhus coriaria	Tanners Sumack
Rhus glabra	Smooth Sumac
Rhus radicans	Poison Vine, Ash, Poison Ivy
*Rhus toxicodendron**	Poison Oak
Rhus typhina	Stag's Horn
Rhus vernix	Varnish Tree, Poison Sumac, Swamp Sumac, Poison Dogwood
Ribes aureum	Golden currant
Ribes cynobasti	Prickly-fruited Gooseberry
Rosa alba var. pleno	Double-white Rose
Rosa arvensis	White Dog Rose
Rosa banksiae	Chinese Rose

Rosa blanda	Hudson's Bay Rose
Rosa carolina	Carolina Rose, Pasture Rose
Rosa centifolia var.	
muscosa	Moss Province Rose
Rosa centifolia var.	
parvifolia	Small-leaved Cabbage Rose
Rosa chinensis	Pale China Rose
Rosa cinnamonea	Cinnamon Rose
Rosa foetida	Single Yellow Austrian Rose, Austrian Brier
Rosa foetida var.	Double Yellow Austrian Rose, Persian Yellow
persiana	Rose
Rosa indica	Indian Rose
Rosa moschata var.	Double Musk Rose; This is a 1600's rose but
plena	now double.
Rosa multiflora	Many-flowered Rose
Rosa pendulina	Alpine Rose
Rosa pendulina var.	
pyrenaica	Pyrenean Rose
Rosa rubrifolia	Red-leaved Rose
Rosa rugosa	Wrinkled-leaved Rose
Rosa sempervirens	Evergreen Rose - The Evergreen Rose referred to in 1600's could be this one.
Rosa virginiana	Shining Leaved American Rose
Rubus odoratus	Flowering Raspberry
Ruscus aculeatus*	Butchersbroom or Prickly Butcher's Broom
Salix babylonica	Babylonian Willow or Weeping Willow
Sambucus nigra	Common European Elder
Sambucus nigra var.	
laciniata	Parsley-leaved Elder
Sambucus pubens	Hairy Elder, American Red Elder
Sambucus racemosa	European Red-berried Elder
Smilax bona-nox	Ciliated or Prickly-leaved Smilax, Saw Brier
Smilax lanceolata	Spear-leaved Smilax
Smilax laurifolia	Bay-leaved Smilax, False China Brier
Smilax rotundifolia	Canadian Round-leaved Smilax
Solanum dulcamara	Woody Nightshade, Bitter Sweet
Sophora japonica*	Scholar Tree
Sophora japonica pendula	Weeping Scholar Tree
Sorbus americana	American Service or Roane Tree, Mountain Ash
Sorbus aucuparia	European Service Tree, European Mountain Ash Rowan
Sorbus hybrida	Bastard Service Tree
Spiraea crenata	Hawthorn-leaved Spiraea
Spiraea hypericifolia	Hypericum-leaved Spiraea
Spiraea salicifolia	Willow-leaved Spiraea
Staphylea trifoliata	Three-leaved Bladder Nut, American Bladder Nut - Bladdernut is referred to in the 1600's but not given genus and species. It is almost certainly this one or S. pinnata.

Stewartia malachodendron *	Stewartia
Styrax grandifolium	Great-leaved Storax Tree or Big-leaf Snowbell
Symphoricarpos albus	
laevigatus	Snowberry
Tamarix gallica	French Tamarisk
Thuja orientalis	Chinese Arbor Vitae
Tilia tomentosa	White or Silver-leaved Linden
Ulmus americana, var.	
pendula	American Drooping Elm
Ulmus carpinifolia	Smooth-leaved Elm
Ulmus carpinifolia, var.	
stricta	Cornish Elm
Ulmus fulva	Red American Elm, Slippery Elm
Ulmus hollandica	Dutch Elm
Ulmus parvifolia	Chinese Elm
Ulmus procera	English Elm
Ulmus pumila	Dwarf Elm
Vaccinium arboreum	Tree Huckleberry, Farkleberry or Sparkleberry
Vaccinium corymbosum	Cluster-flowered Huckle-berry, Highbush, Swamp Blueberry, Whortleberry
Vaccinium myrtillus	European Huckleberry, Bill-berry, Whortleberry
Vaccinium oxycoccos	European Cranberry, Bog-berry
Vaccinium stamineum	Green-twigged Huckle-berry, Deerberry
Viburnum alnifolium	Alder-leaved Viburnum, Hobble Bush, American Wayfaring Tree
Viburnum laevigatum	Cassioberry Bush
Viburnum nudum	Oval-leaved Viburnum, Smooth Withe Rod
Viburnum tomentosum var.	Japanese Snowball - Not too popular until
sterile	Thomas Meehan's nursery began to specialize in this plant in 1853.
Viburnum tinus	Lauristinus
Vinca major	Large Periwinkle
Wisteria sinensis	Chinese Wisteria
Xanthoriza simplicissima	Shrub Yellow Root
Yucca gloriosa	Mound Lily Yucca, Spanish Dagger
Zanthoxylum clava-herulis	Ash-leaved Tooth-ack Tree, Hercules Club

VEGETABLES AND FIELD CROPS - 1776-1850

Agaricus campestris	Mushroom
Allium ascalonicum	Shallot
Allium scorodopnasum	Rocambole, Giant Garlic
Apium graveolens var.	
rapaceum	Celeriac, Turnep-rooted Celery
Arachis hypogoea	Ground Nut, Goober, Peanut
Armoracia rusticana	Horse Radish
Atriplex hortensis	Orach, English Lamb's-quarter - 2 varieties: Large Green-leaved, Large Red-leaved

Brassica oleracea var. acephala and other varieties	Kale, Borecole
Brassica oleracea var. gemmifera	Brussels Sprouts
Brassica oleracea var. italica	Italian Broccoli
Cichorium endivia	Green-curled, White-curled, or Broad Leaved Endive
Cucumis anguria	Round Prickly Cucumber, India or Bur Gherkin
Crambe maritima	Sea Kale, Cabbage
Ipomaea batatas	Sweet Potatoe
Lycopersicon esculentum	Tomatoes or Love-apple
Nasturtium officinale	Water Cress
Onyza sativa	Rice
Rumex scutatus	Round-leaved Sorrel
Scorzonera hispanica	Scorzonera, Black Salsify
Solanum melongena	Egg Plant
Tragapogon porrifolius	Salsafy, Vegetable Oyster
Vicia faba	Common Garden Bean, McMahon lists 14 varieties +

HERBS: AROMATIC, CULINARY AND MEDICINAL - 1776-1850

Achillea ageratum	Sweet Yarrow
Althea officinalis	Marsh Mallow
Anagalis arvensis	Pimpernel, Poor Mans Weatherglass
Apium graveolens	Smallage
Aristolochia serpentaria	Virginia Snake-root
Artemisia absinthium	Wormwood
Artemisia vulgaris	Common Mugwort
Chelidonium majus	Celandine
Chenepodium ambrosioides (probably)	Wormseed, Goosefoot, Mexican Tea
Cnicus benedictus	Carduus Benedictus or Blessed Thistle
Cochlearia officinalis	Scurvy-grass
Eupatorium perfoliatum	Ague-weed, Thoroughwort, Common Boneset
Lithospermum officinale	Gromwell
Majorana onites	Pot Marjoram
Mandragora sp. (probably)	Mandrake
Marrubium vulgare	Horehound
Papaver somniferum	Opium Poppy
Rheum palmatum	Rhubarb, True Turkey
Ricinus communis	Castor-oil Nut, Palma Christi, Castor Bean
Satureja hortensis	Summer Savory - referred to before 1700, but not by species
Satureja montana	Winter Savory - probably grown in the 1600's
Spigelia marilandica	Carolina Pink-root

Stachys officinalis	Wood Betony, Woundwort
Thymus vulgaris	Common Thyme
Trigonella foenum graecum	Fenugreek
Urtica dioica	Stinging Nettle
Valerianella olitoria	Corn-sallad

FLOWERS - 1850-1900

Achillea fillipendulina	Fernleaf Yarrow
Achillea millefolium rosea	Yarrow or Milfoil Variety
Achillea ptarmica, fl. pl. *	Sneezewort
Achillea tomentosa	Downy Yarrow, Wooly Yarrow
Aconitum autumnale	Autumn Monk's-hood
Acorus calamus	Sweet Flag
Adonis vernalis *	Spring Adonis
Ailanthus altissima	Tree-of-heaven - Keep a young one pruned to the roots every spring to have very large foliage for garden. So also with Paulownia. Henderson.
Ajuga reptans var. alba	Carpet Bugle, Bugle-weed
Alternanthera bettzickiana	Alternanthera
Althea rosea *	Hollyhock
Alyssum repens var. wierzbickii	Alyssum
Alyssum saxatile	Golden Tuft, Gold-dust, Basket-of-gold, Rock Madwort
Alysum saxatile var. compactum	Dwarf Golden Tuft
Amaranthus hybridus var. hypochondriacus	Prince's Feather
Amaranthus tricolor var. salicifolius *	
Anemone blanda	Windflower
Anemone caroliniana	Windflower
Anemone japonica	Japanese Anemone
Anemone pulsatilla	European Pasque-flower, Pasque-flower
Anemone quinquefolia	Wood Anemone
Anemone sylvestris	Snowdrop Wind-flower
Anthemis tinctoria	Yellow Chamomile, Golden Marguerite
Anthericum liliago	St. Bernard's Lily
Antirrhinum glutinosum	Snapdragon
Aquilegia canadensis *	Canada Columbine
Arabis alpina	Alpine Rock Cress
Arenaria verna	Spring Sandwort
Armeria maritima var. elongata *	Sea Pink, Thrift
Aruncus sylvester *	Goat's Beard
Arundo donax	Green-leaved Bamboo, Giant Reed
Asclepias tuberosa *	Butterfly Weed or Swallow-wort

Asparagus sprengeri	
Asperula odorata	Common Woodruff, Sweet Woodruff
Asphodelus luteus *	Asphodel, King's Spear
Aster novae-angliae *	New England Aster
Aster ptarmicoides	White Upland Aster
Astilbe japonica	
Aubrieta sp.	Half Dozen or More sp.
Baptisia australis	Blue False Indigo
Bergenia cordifolia	Heart-leaved Saxifrage
Bulbocodium vernum	Spring Meadow Saffron
Caladium bicolor	Caladium
Calla palustris	Water Arum
Campanula carpatica *	Carpet Bell-flower
Campanula isophylla var. alba	Bellflower
Campanula medium *	Canterbury Bells - singles & doubles
Campanula rotundifolia	Harebell
Carica papaya *	Papaya, Pawpaw - First season for foliage
Cassia marilandica	American Senna, Wild Senna
Cerastium tomentosum	Snow-in-summer
Ceratostigma plumbaginoides	Leadwort
Chionodoxa lucilia	Glory-of-the-snow
Chrysanthemum maximum	Max Chrysanthemums or Daisy - ". . . Known in many forms, as King Edward VII, Chrysanthemum daisy, Shasta daisy, Glory of the Wayside, . . .". Parsons
Chrysanthemum sp. *	Japanese & Chinese Chrysanthemums
Chrysanthemum uliginosum	Giant Daisy, "white moon-penny daisies"
Clematis integrifolia *	Virgin's Bower
Cobaea scandens	
Colchicum autumnale *	Autumn Crocus
Convallaria majalis *	Lily-of-the-valley
Coreopsis lanceolata *	Tickseed
Cortaderia selloana	Pampas Grass
Corydalis nobilis	Corydalis
Crocus vernus *	Crocus
Cymbalaria muralis	Kenilworth Ivy
Cyperus alternifolius	Umbrella Plant
Cyperus papyrus	Papyrus
Cypripedium sp. *	Moccasin Flower
Dahlia sp.	Dahlias, esp. singles which "have been deservedly increasing in reputation of late". Parsons
Datura humilis flava florepleno	A horticultural variety of D. Metel "large, yellow, sweet-scented flowers".
Datura metel *	Datura
Datura metel alba plena	
Datura meteloides	
Delphinium cheilanthum var. formosum	Beautiful Larkspur, Garland Larkspur
Delphinium elatum *	Tall Larkspur, Candle or Bee Larkspur

116

Delphinium grandiflorum	Bouquet Larkspur, Double-flowering Larkspur
Delphinium nudicaule	Red Larkspur
*Dianthus barbatus**	Sweet-william
*Dianthus deltoides**	Maiden's Pink
*Dianthus plumarius**	Garden Pink, Cushion Pink, Cottage Pink
Dicentra eximia	Plumy Bleeding-heart
Dicentra spectabilis	Bleeding Heart
*Dictamnus albus**	Gas Plant, Dittany, Fraxinella, Burning Bush
*Digitalis purpurea**	Foxglove
*Dodecatheon meadia**	American Cowslip, Shooting Star
*Epimedium grandiflorum**	Barrenwort - especially var. alba
*Eranthis hyemalis**	Winter Aconite
Erianthus ravennae	Plume-grass, Ravenna-grass
*Eryngium alpinum**	Alpine Eryngium
Eucalyptus globulus	Blue Gum - First season for foliage
Euphorbia corollata	Flowering Spurge
Ferns	Especially native species in naturalistic settings.
Ficus elastica	Rubber Plant
*Filipendula hexapetala var. florepleno**	Dropwort, "old & favorite plant"
Filipendula palmata	
Filipendula ulmaria	Meadow-sweet, Queen of the Meadow
Gaillardia aristata	Gaillardias, have been much improved recently. Parsons
Galanthus elwesii	Giant Snowdrop
*Galanthus nivalis**	Snowdrop
Gaultonia candicans	Giant Summer Hyacinth
*Gentiana acaulis**	Stemless Gentian
Geranium sanguineum	Blood-red Geranium
Grevillea robusta	Silk Oak - First season for foliage
Gunnera manicata	Gunnera
Gypsophila paniculata	Babys Breath
*Helianthus sp. **	Double Perennial Sunflower
*Helleborus niger**, *H. niger altifolius*	Christmas Rose
*Hemerocallis flava**	Day Lily
*Hepatica americana**	Liver-leaf
*Hesperis matronalis**	Double Rocket - Double purple & Double white
*Hibiscus moscheutos**	Marsh Rose-mallow
Hosta caerulea	Blue Plantain
Hosta lancifolia var. albomarginata	
Hosta plantaginea	Plantain Lily, Fragrant Plantain, Day Lily
*Houstonia coerulea**	Bluets
*Hyacinthus orientalis**	Many varieties
Iberis corifolia	Corris-leaved Perennial Candy Tuft
*Ipomaea purpurea**	Morning Glory
*Iris cristata**	Crested Iris

*Iris germanica**	German Iris - ". . . by hybridization fine varieties with a great range of beautiful combinations of color have been secured."
*Iris germanica var. florentina**	Florentine Iris, Orris Root
Iris kaempferi	Japanese Iris
*Iris pumila**	
Iris reticulata	Golden Netted Iris
*Iris sibirica**	Siberian Iris
Kniphofia uvaria	Tritoma, Kniphofia, Red-hot Poker Plant, Torch Lily
*Lathyrus latifolius**	Everlasting Pea
Leontopodium alpinum	Edelweiss
*Leucojum vernum**	Spring Snowflake
Liatris pycnostachya	Kansas Gay-feather
*Liatris spicata**	Button Snakeroot, Blazing Star, Gay Feather
Ligularia japonica	Groundsel
Lilium auratum	Goldband Lily
*Lilium canadense**	Meadow Lily
Lilium canadense var. coccineum	
*Lilium candidum**	Madonna Lily
Lilium pardalinum	Leopard Lily
Lilium parryi	Lemon Lily
*Linum perenne**	Perennial Flax
*Lilium pomponium**	Pomponian Lily, Lesser Turks-cap Lily
Lilium pyrenaicum	Yellow Turban Lily, Yellow Turks-cap
Lilium speciosum	Showy Japanese Lily
*Lilium superbum**	Turk's-cap Lily
Lilium tigrinum	Tiger Lily
Lilium tigrinum var. splendens	Tiger Lily
Limonium latifolium	Woundwort
*Lobelia cardinalis**	Cardinal Flower
*Lupinus sp.**	Hardy Lupines
*Lychnis chalcedonica**	Scarlet Lychnis or Maltese Cross - "It has been neglected for much less showy summer flowers". Parsons
Lychnis chalcedonica, fl. pl.	Double Scarlet Lychnis
Lychnis viscaria var. splendens	German Catchfly
Lycoris squamigera	Hall's Amaryllis
*Lythrum salicaria**	Purple Loosestrife
Macleaya cordata	Plume Poppy
Malva alcea	Garden Mallow
Malva moschata alba	Musk Mallow
Miscanthus sinensis var. gracillimus	

Miscanthus sinensis var. variegatus	
Miscanthus probably sinensis var. zebrinus	Zebra Grass
Mitchella repens	Partridge-berry
*Monarda didyma**	Bee Balm, Oswego Tea
*Muscari sp.**	Grape Hyacinths
Narcissus imcomparabilis	Many forms
*Narcissus odorus**	Campernelle Jonquil
*Narcissus poeticus**	Poet's Narcissus, Pheasant's Eye
*Narcissus pseudo-narcissus**	Daffodil or Daffodowndilly
*Narcissus pseudo-narcissus form bicolor**	Two-coloured Narcissus
Narcissus pseudo-narcissus form maximus	Daffodil, form
*Narcissus tazetta form bicolor**	Two-coloured Narcissus
Narcissus triandrus var. cernuus	Angels-Tears, variety
Nelumbium nelumbo	East Indian Lotus
*Nelumbium pentapetalum**	Yellow Lotus
*Nepeta hederacea**	Ground Ivy, Gill-over-the-ground, Field Balm
Nicotiana alata var. grandiflora	Nicotiana
Nierembergia rivularis	White-cup
*Nymphaea alba, var. candidissima**	European White Water Lily Variety
Nymphaea capensis var. zanzibarensis azurea	Cape Blue Water Lily, variety
Nymphaea capensis var. zanzibarensis rosea	Cape Blue Water Lily, variety
Nymphaea devoniensis X	
Nymphaea lotus	Egyptian Sacred Lotus, White Lotus of Egypt
*Nymphaea odorata var. rosea**	Fragrant Water Lily, Cape Cod Pink Lily
Nymphoides indicum	Water Snowflake
Oenothera missouriensis	Evening Primrose
Oenothera speciosa	Evening Primrose
Opuntia compressa	Western Prickly Pear
Opuntia sp.	Prickly Pear, Indian Fig Type
Orontium aquaticum	Golden Club
Osmunda regalis	Royal Fern
*Paeonia sp.**	Peony
*Paeonia tenuifolia, fl. pl.**	Peony
Papaver bracteatum	Poppy
*Papaver orientale**	Oriental Poppy
Papaver nudicaule var. croceum	Iceland Poppy
*Papaver sp.**	Annual Poppies
Paulownia tomentosa	Royal Paulownia, Empress Tree - Henderson

recommends keeping a young tree pruned back to the roots each spring so as to have the very attractive, large foliage for the garden.

Pelargonium peltatum	Ivy-leaved Geranium
Pelargonium zonale	Horseshoe Geranium
Pennisetum ruppellii	Fountain Grass
Pennisetum villosum	Grass
Penstemon coboea	Beard Tongue
Penstemon torreyi	Beard Tongue
Perilla frutenscens var.	
crispa	Perilla
Petalostemum decumbens	Prarie Clover
Petunia hybrida	Common Garden Petunia
Phalaris arundinacea var. picta	Ribbon Grass
Phlox decussata	Summer Perennial Phlox - decussata is a name applied to horticultural forms of Phlox paniculata*, P. maculata*, P. suffruticosa. Bailey
Phlox nivalis var. alba	Trailing Phlox, Fine-leaved Phlox
Phlox procumbens	
Phlox stellaria	Starry Phlox
Phlox subulata*	Ground Phlox, Moss Pink
Phyllostachys sp.	Bamboo - Phyllostachys niger henonis, P. nigra and P. viridi-glaucescens, are especially hardy.
Piqueria trinervia var.	
variegata	
Platycodon grandiflorum	Large Bell-flower, Balloon Flower
Polygonatum sp. *	Solomons Seal
Primula sp. *	Hardy Primulas
Primula japonica	Japanese Primrose
Primula vulgaris*	Common, Wild English Primrose - S. Parsons recommends this but says it is seldom grown.
Ranunculus speciosus, fl. pl	Bachelor's-button, Creeping Buttercup
Rheum palmatum	Giant Rhubarb
Ricinus communis*	Castor-oil Plant
Rubus odoratus	Purple-flowering Raspberry - "old well-known plant of the highest excellence". Parsons
Rudbeckia laciniata var.	
hortensia	Coneflower, Golden Glow - Fls. double
Rudbeckia maxima	Large Cone-flower
Salvia pratensis	Meadow-sage
Sanguinaria canadensis*	Bloodroot
Saponaria ocymoides*	Basil-leaved Soapwort
Sarracenia sp. *	Pitcher Plants
Saxifraga longifolia	Saxifrage, Rockfoil
Saxifraga sp. *	Saxifrage, Rockfoil
Scabiosa caucasica	Scabious, Mourning Bride, Pincushion-flower
Scilla sp. *	Scilla
Sedum acre	Common Stone-crop

Sedum sieboldii	
Sedum spectabile	
Sempervivum arachnoideum *	Cobweb House Leek
Sempervivum calcareum	Houseleek
Sempervivum tectorum	Common House-leek, Roof Houseleek, Hen-and-chickens, Old-man-and-woman
Senecio cineraria var. candidissimus	Cineraria (White Leaved)
Silene caroliniana *	Wild Pink, Penn. Catchfly
Silene virginica *	Fire Pink
Silphium laciniatum *	Compass Plant
Solidago canadensis	Goldenrod
Solidago rigida	
Solidago shortii	
Stipa pennata	Spear Grass, Feather Grass
Stokesia laevis *	Stokes Aster
Symplocarpus foetidus	Skunk Cabbage
Tetrapanax papyriferum	
Thalictrum glaucum	Meadow-rue - "fine large yellow-flowered sort with handsome leaves which grow three to five feet high". Parsons
Thymus serpyllum var. aureus, also var. argenteus & variegatus	Variegated Thyme, Mother-of-thyme, Creeping Thyme
Tradescantia virginica *	Spiderwort
Trillium sp. *	Trillium
Trollius europaeus	European Globe Flower
Tropaeolum majus *	Nasturtium
Tropaeolum majus probably var. Burpeei	Double Nasturtium, Golden Gleam Nasturtium
Tulipa sp. *	Tulips
Tunica saxifraga	Rock Tunica
Typha latifolia *	Cat-tails
Verbascum olympicum	Mullein
Verbascum sp. *	Verbascum, Mullein
Verbena hortensis *	Garden Verbena
Vernonia noveboracensis	N.Y. Iron-weed
Veronica gentianoides	Gentian Leaved Speedwell
Veronica longifolia var. subsessilis	Best of the Speedwells
Veronica spuria	"Better than Gentianoides." Parsons
Vinca minor *	Trailing Vinca
Viola cornuta	Horned Violet
Viola pedata *	Bird's-foot Violet
Xerophyllum asphodeloides	Turkey's Beard
Yucca filamentosa *	Yucca
Zantedeschia sp.	Calla
Zea mays var. curarua & var. japonica	Corn for Ornamentation

BEDDING PLANTS - 1850-1900

Abutilon hybridum var.	
souvenir de bonn	Abutilon, Variegated Leaved
Acalypha wilkesiana var.	
macrophylla	Copper-leaf
Acalypha wilkesiana var.	
musaica	Copper-leaf
Agave americana	Century Plant - for pots and bedding
Ageratum sp.	Dwarf Blue Ageratum
Alternanthera amoena	Telanthera
Alternanthera bettzickiana	Telanthera
Alternanthera bettzickiana	
var. aurea	
Alternanthera bettzickiana	
var. aurea nana	
Alternanthera versicolor	Copper Alternanthera
Begonia semperflorens	Begonia Vernon
Begonia tuberhybrida	Tuberous Begonia
Canna ehmanni	Canna
Canna ehemannii X C. glauca	
& others	French Canna, Dwarf
Canna indica	Indian Shot, many varieties
Centaurea gymnocarpa	Dusty Miller
Chrysanthemum parthenium	
var. aureum	Feverfew or Golden Feather
Chrysanthemum sp. *	Daisies
Coleus blumei var.	
golden bedder	
Coleus blumei var.	
kirkpatrick	
Coleus blumei var.	
vershaffeltii	
Coleus sp.	Varieties of diverse sorts
Colocasia esculenta	Elephant Ear, Taro, Eddo, Dasheen
Cordyline indivisa	
Cuphea platycentra	Cigar Flower
Echeveria gibbiflora var.	
metallica	
Echeveria secunda var.	
glauca	
Gladiolus hortulanus	Gladiolus, Sword Lily, Garden Gladioli, Hortulan
Iresine sp.	
Lantana camara var.	
hybrida	Dwarf Lantana
Lobelia erinus	
*Lobularia maritima**	Sweet Alyssum
Lobularia maritima (variegated)	Alyssum, variegated
Musa ensete	Banana Plant, Abyssinian Banana

122

Nierembergia sp.
Oxalis corniculata var.
   atropurpurea
Pelargonium sp. — Geranium, Doubles & Singles
Pelargonium sp. — Silver-leaved Geranium
Pelargonium zonale — Horseshoe Geranium
Piqueria trinervia
*Ricinus communis** — Castor-oil Plant
Salvia splendens — Scarlet Salvia
*Santolina chamaecyparissus** — Lavender-cotton
Sedum acre — Common Stone-crop
Senecio leucostachys — Centauria, Dusty Miller
Thymus serpyllum var. variegatus — Variegated Thyme
*Tropaeolum majus** — Garden Nasturtium
Tulipa gesneriana — Tulip varieties: La Belle Alliance, excellent red; Artus, excellent red; Pottebaker, white; Yellow Prince, yellow; Canary Bird, yellow
Tulipa suaveolens — Duc Van Tholl Tulip, Red-dwarf
Vinca rosea — Madagascar Periwinkle
Viola tricolor var. hortensis — Pansies

TREES, SHRUBS & VINES - 1850-1900

Abies alba var. pendula — Weeping Silver Fir
Abies cephalonica — Greek Fir
Abies concolor — White Fir
Abies nordmannia — Nordmann Fir
Abies sibirica — Siberian Silver Fir
Acanthopanax sieboldianus — Five-leaf Aralia
Acer japonicum — Fullmoon Maple, "fine red flowers"
Acer japonicum aureum — Yellow Leaves
*Acer palmatum** — Japanese Maple, there are many varieties
Acer palmatum ornatum — Spider-leaf Japanese Maple
Acer palmatum sanguineum — Scarlet Japanese Maple
*Acer pennsylvanicum** — Striped Maple, Moosewood
*Acer platanoides** — Norway Maple
Acer platanoides 'lorbergii'
Acer platanoides 'schwedleri' — Swedler Maple
*Acer pseudo-platanus** — Sycamore Maple
Acer pseudo-platanus var. leopoldii
Acer pseudo-platanus var. purpureum — Also many other varieties: Silver Variegated, Golden Tinged, Golden, Striped, etc.
*Acer rubrum** — Red, Scarlet, Swamp Maple
Actinidia chinensis — China Gooseberry
*Adlumia fungosa** — Mountain Fringe, Climbing Fumitory, Allegheny Vine
Aesculus carnea — Red-flowering Horse Chestnut - "perhaps finest of all"

123

*Aesculus hippocastanum**	Horse Chestnut
Aesculus parviflora	Bottlebrush Buckeye, Dwarf Horse Chestnut
*Akebia quinata**	Five-leaf Akebia, not introduced until 1845.
*Albizzia julibrissin**	Virginia Silk
Albizzia lophantha	Plume Albizia
Alnus glutinosa var.	
imperialis	Cut-leaved Alder, Black Alder
*Amorpha sp.**	False Indigo - "small purplish flowers in dense terminal flattish clusters during early summer".
Ampelopsis brevipedunculata	Porcelain Ampelopsis
Anemone hupehensis japonica	Autumn Flowering Anemone
*Aralia elata**	Japanese Angelica Tree
*Aralia spinosa**	Hercules Club
Areca sp.	Feather-palm
*Aristolochia durior**	Dutchman's Pipe
Aucuba japonica	Japanese Aucuba
Berberis thunbergii	Japanese Barberry
Berberis thunbergii var.	
atropurpurea	Purple Berberry, Japanese Barberry
*Betula lenta**	Black Birch
*Betula lutea**	Yellow Birch
*Betula papyrifera**	White Birch, Canoe or Paper Birch
*Betula pendula**	Common European Birch, European White Birch, Weeping Birch
Betula pendula var. purpurea	Purple European Birch
Bougainvillea glabra	Bougainvillea
Bougainvillea spectabilis	Bougainvillea
Buddleja davidii	Common Buddleia, Summer Lilac - Introduced about 1890.
Buxus microphylla	Little-leaf Box
Buxus sempervirens var.	
arborescens	Tree Box
Buxus sempervirens var.	
suffruticosa or another dwarf	
*form**	Dwarf Box
Callicarpa dichotoma	Beauty-berry
Callicarpa japonica	Japanese Beauty-berry
*Calycanthus floridus**	Sweet-scented Shrub, Carolina Allspice
Campsis grandiflora	Chinese Trumpet-creeper
*Campsis radicans**	Trumpet-creeper
*Carpinus betulus**	European Hornbeam
*Carpinus caroliniana**	American Hornbeam
Caryota sp.	Fish-tail Palm
*Castanea dentata**	American Chestnut
Catalpa bignonioides	Southern Catalpa, Common Catalpa, Indian Bean
Catalpa bignonioides var. aurea	Golden Catalpa
Catalpa bignonioides var. nana	Dwarf Catalpa - Catalpa big. var. nana "is the C. Bungii of horticulturists".

124

Cedrus atlantica*	Atlas Cedar
Cedrus libani*	Cedar of Lebanon
Celastrus orbiculatus	Asiatic Bittersweet Vine
Celastrus scandens*	Bitter-sweet
Cercidiphyllum japonicum	Katsura-tree
Cercis chinensis	Chinese Redbud
Chaenomeles lagenaria*	Japanese Quince, Flowering Quince
Chamaecyparis obtusa	Hinoki False Cypress
Chamaecyparis pisifera	Sawara False Cypress
Chamaecyparis pisifera aurea	Golden Sawara False Cypress
Chamaecyparis pisifera var. plumosa	
Chamaecyparis pisifera filifera pendula	
Chamaecyparis pisifera squarrosa	Moss Sawara False Cypress
Chionanthus retusus	Fringe Tree
Chionathus virginica*	White Fringe Tree
Cladrastis lutea*	American Yellow-wood
Clematis flammula	Sweet-scented Clematis
Clematis X jackmanii	Jackman Clematis - "perhaps the best". Parsons
Clematis X jackmanii hybrids	Introduced before 1900. Gypsy Queen, Madame Edouard Andre, Mrs. Cholmondeley
Clematis lanuginosa	Ningpo Clematis
Clematis lanuginosa hybrids	Introduced before 1890. Perle d' Azur, Lady Caroline Neville, Lord Neville, Ramona, W. E. Gladstone
Clematis paniculata	Sweet Autumn Clematis
Clematis paniculata var. dioscoreifolia	
Clematis tangutica	Golden Clematis - introduced in 1890.
Clematis virginiana*	Virgin's Bower
Clerodendron bungei	Rose Glory-bower
Clerodendrum trichotomum	Harlequin Glory-bower
Clethra alnifolia*	Sweet Pepper Bush
Colutea sp.*	Bladder Senna
Cornus alba var. sibirica	Red-twigged Dogwood
Cornus florida*	White-flowering Dogwood
Cornus florida pendula	
Cornus florida rubra*	Pink Dogwood
Cornus kousa	Kousa or Japanese Dogwood
Cornus kousa (variegated)	Grown in this country before the species itself.
Corylus maxima purpurea	Purple Hazelnut, Filbert
Cotinus coggygria*	Purple Fringe
Cotoneaster horizontalis	Rock-spray - Not used until after 1880.
Crataegus crus-galli*	Cock-spur Thorn
Cryptomeria japonica	Cryptomeria
Cryptomeria japonica elegans	Plume Cryptomeria

Cryptomeria japonica forma variegata	Cryptomeria
Cycas revoluta	Sago Palm
Cytisus praecox	Warminster Broom
*Cytisus scoparia**	Scotch Broom
Daphne genkwa	Daphne
*Daphne cneorum**	Rose Daphne
*Daphne mezereum**	Daphne, Mezereum
Deutzia gracilis	Slender Deutzia
Deutzia scabra plena	Double-flowered Deutzia
Dioscorea batatas	Cinnamon Vine or Chinese Yam
Diospyros kaki	Japanese Persimmon or Kaki
*Diospyros virginiana**	American Persimmon
Dracaena draco	Dragon Tree
*Elaeagnus angustifolia**	Russian Olive
Enkianthus campanulatus	Redvein Enkianthus
Erica carnea	Spring Heath
Euonymus alatus	Winged Euonymus
*Euonymus europaeus**	European Euonymus, Spindle Tree
Euonymus fortunei vegetus	Evergreen Bittersweet
*Exochorda racemosa**	Pearl Bush
*Fagus grandifolia**	American Beech
*Fagus sylvatica**	European Beech
Fagus sylvatica var. atropunicea	Purple Beech
Fagus sylvatica pendula	Weeping European Beech, Weeping Beech
Forsythia suspensa	Weeping Forsythia
Forsythia suspensa fortunii	Forsythia
Forsythia viridissima	
*Fothergilla gardenii**	Dwarf Fothergilla
*Fraxinus excelsior**	European Ash
Genista tinctoria	Dyers Greenweed
*Ginkgo biloba**	Ginkgo
Ginko biloba form variegata	
*Gleditsia tricanthos**	Honey Locust
Glyptostrobus pensilis	Chinese Cypress
*Gymnocladus dioicus**	Kentucky Coffee Tree
*Halesia carolina**	Snowdrop Tree, Silver-bell
Hamamelis mollis	Chinese Witch-hazel
*Hamamelis virginiana**	Witch Hazel
*Hibiscus syriacus**	Althea
*Hibiscus syriacus, fl. pl. **	Double Flowering Althea
Hydrangea paniculata grandiflora	Peegee Hydrangea
Hydrangea petiolaris	Climbing Hydrangea
Hydrangea quercifolia	Oak-leaved Hydrangea
Hypericum patulum	
Ilex cornuta	Chinese Holly
*Ilex crenata**	Japanese Holly
*Ilex opaca**	American Holly

126

Itea virginica *	Virginian Willow or Sweet Spire
Jasminum nudiflorum	Jasmine
Juniperus communis var. *depressa*	Canadian Juniper
Juniperus communis var. *hibernica*	Irish Juniper
Juniperus formosana	Weeping Juniper
Juniperus horizontalis	Creeping Juniper
Juniperus procumbens	Procumbent Juniper
Juniperus virginiana *	Red Cedar
Juniperus virginiana glauca	Silver Red Cedar
Juniperus virginiana *pendula*	Weeping Red Cedar
Juniperus virginiana var. *venusta*	Red Cedar Variety
Juniperus sabina *	Savin Juniper
Juniperus squamata	Himalayan Juniper
Kalmia latifolia *	Broad-leaved Laurel, Mountain Laurel
Kerria japonica	Kerria
Koelreuteria *	Golden Rain Tree
Laburnum anagyroides *	Common Laburnum
Laburnum X watereri	Waterer Laburnum
Larix decidua *	European Larch
Larix decidua pendula	Weeping Larch
Larix laricina	American Larch, Tamarack or Hackmatack
Larix leptolepsis	Japanese Larch, Japanese Leptolepsis
Larix pendula X	Weeping Larch
Lespedeza bicolor	Shrub Bush-clover
Ligustrum amurense	Amur Privet
Ligustrum ovalifolium	California Privet
Liquidambar styraciflua *	Sweet Gum or Liquid Ambar
Liriodendron tulipifera *	Tulip Tree
Lonicera canadensis	Fly Honeysuckle
Lonicera fragrantissima	Winter Honeysuckle
Lonicera gracilipes	Spangle Honeysuckle
Lonicera japonica halliana	Hall's Honeysuckle
Lonicera japonica var. *repens*	Japanese Honeysuckle Variety
Lonicera maacki	Amur Honeysuckle
Lonicera morrowii	Morrow Honeysuckle
Lonicera periclymenum var. *belgica*	Dutch Woodbine - "Belgian, or striped monthly (red & white)", "perhaps best known & most gen. popular".
Lonicera sempervirens *	Trumpet Honeysuckle
Lonicera tartarica *	Tartarian Honeysuckle
Lycium barbarum	Box Thorn, Matrimony Vine
Magnolia cordata	Yellow Cucumber Tree
Magnolia denudata *	Yulan Magnolia
Magnolia kobus	Kobus magnolia
Magnolia liliflora var.	

127

gracilis	Lily Magnolia
*Magnolia macrophylla**	Big Leaf Magnolia
Magnolia obovata	Whiteleaf Japanese Maple
Magnolia soulangeana X*	Saucer Magnolia
Magnolia soulangeana var.	
norbetiana	
Magnolia stellata	Star Magnolia
*Magnolia tripetala**	Umbrella Magnolia
*Magnolia virginiana**	White Swamp Magnolia
*Mahonia aquifolium**	Oregon Holly-grape
Mahonia bealei	Leatherleaf Mahonia
Malus floribunda	Japanese Crab Apple
Malus ioensis plena	Bechtel Crab Apple - not used until after 1888.
Malus sargentii	Sargent Crab Apple - not until after 1892.
Malus sieboldii	Toringo Crab or Dwarf Crab
*Menispermum canadense**	Moon-seed
Michelia fuscata	Banana Shrub
Morus alba pendula	Tea's Mulberry
Musa ensete	Banana
*Myrica cerifera**	Bayberry, Wax Myrtle
Opuntia bigelivii	Jumping Cholla, Teddy-bear Cactus
Osmanthus heterophyllus	Osmanthus
*Oxydendrum arboreum**	Sour-wood, Sorrel-tree
Pachysandra terminalis	Japanese Spurge - not used until after 1882.
*Parthenocissus quinquefolia**	Virginia Creeper
Parthenocissus tricuspidata	Boston-ivy, Japan Ivy
Parthenocissus tricuspidata	
var. veitchi	
*Paulownia tomentosa**	Empress Tree
Phellodendron amurense	Amur Cork-tree
*Philadelphus coronarius**	Sweet Mock-orange
Philadelphus coronarius var.	
aureus	Fine, Dwarf, Golden Var.
Philadelphus grandiflorus	Big Scentless Mock-orange
Philadelphus laxus	Drooping Mock-orange
Phoenix canariensis	Canary Island Date
Photinia villosa	Oriental Photinia
Physocarpus opulifolius	
var. luteus	Ninebark Variety
Picea abies inversa	Weeping Norway Spruce
Picea abies virgata elata	Norway Spruce Variety
Picea engelmannii	Engelmann Spruce
*Picea glauca**	American White Spruce
Picea glauca var. gloriosa	Glory of the Spruce - "warm golden tint in the midst of its young green". Parsons
*Picea orientalis**	Oriental Spruce
Picea pungens	Blue Spruce
Pieris japonica	Japanese Pieris
*Pinus cembra**	Swiss Stone Pine

128

Pinus mugo mughus *	Dark Mughus Pine, Mugo Pine
Pinus mugo var. compacta	Mughus Compacta
Pinus aristata	Bristle-cone Pine
Pinus densiflora	Japanese Red Pine
Pinus lambertiana	Sugar Pine
Pinus nigra *	Austrian Pine
Pinus strobus nana	Dwarf White Pine
Pinus strobus var.	
glauca dwarf form	Light Blue Dwarf White Pine
Pinus sylvestris nana	Dwarf Scotch Pine
Pinus thunbergii	Japanese Black Pine
Platanus occidentalis *	Sycamore, Large Buttonwood
Populus nigra var. italica *	Lombardy Poplar
Populus tremuloides *	Quaking Aspen
Prunus avium 'plena'	Double-flowered Mazzard Cherry - "Old White double-flowering Cherry
Prunus cerasifera atropurpurea	Pissard Plum - used after 1885
Prunus maritima *	Beach Plum
Prunus persica fl. pl.	Double Flowered Peach
Prunus sargentii	Sargent Cherry
Prunus subhirtella pendula	Weeping Higan Cherry, Weeping Japanese Cherry
Prunus triloba	Flowering Almond
Pseudolarix amabilis	Golden Larch
Pseudotsuga menziesii	Douglas Fir
Pueraria thunbergiana	Kudzu-vine
Pyracantha coccinea *	Scarlet Firethorn
Quercus alba *	White Oak
Quercus borealis *	Red Oak
Quercus coccinea *	Scarlet Oak
Quercus montana	Chestnut Oak
Quercus palustris	Pin Oak
Quercus phellos *	Willow Oak
Quercus robur	English Oak
Quercus robur concordia	Golden Oak - "leaves bright yellow"
Quercus robur var.	
fastigiata	Pyramidal English Oak
Quercus robur pendula	Weeping English Oak
Quercus sp. *	Oaks
Rhododendron amoenum	Amoena Azalea
Rhododendron arborescens	Sweet Azalea
Rhododendron calendulaceum *	Flame Azalea
Rhododendron canadense *	Rhodora - "choice but not very often grown". Parsons
Rhododendron catawbiense *	Catawba Rhododendron
Rhododendron fortunei	Fortune's Rhododendron
Rhododendron X gandavense	Ghent Azalea
Rhododendron kaempferi	Torch Azalea - not used until after 1892.
Rhododendron maximum *	Rosebay Rhododendron
Rhododendron mucronulatum	Korean Rhododendron

Rhododendron molle	"comparatively recent introduction"
*Rhododendron nudiflorum**	Pinxter Flower
Rhododendron obtusum var.	
amoenum	Flowers double, Hose-in-hose
Rhododendron occidentale	Western Azalea
Rhododendron vaseyi	Pinkshell Azalea
*Rhododendron viscosum**	White Swamp Honeysuckle
Rhodotypos tetropetala	Jetbead
*Rhus aromatica**	Fragrant Sumac
Rosa cathayensis var.	
crimson rambler	Crimson Rambler
*Rosa eglanteria**	Sweetbrier
Rosa multiflora	Multiflora Rose
Rosa noisettiana	Noisette or Champrey Rose
Rosa odorata	Tea Rose
*Rosa rugosa**	Rugosa Rose
Rosa wichuraiana	Memorial Rose - Introduced in 1891.
*Rubus odoratus**	Flowering Raspberry
*Salix babylonica**	Weeping Willow
Salix babylonica var.	
aurea	Golden Willow
Salix caprea	Goat Willow, Sallow Willow
Salix caprea pendula	Weeping Kilmarnock Willow
Salix pentandra	Laurel-leaved Willow
Sambucus nigra aurea	European Elder
Sciadopitys verticillata	Japanese Umbrella Pine
Sciadopitys verticillata	
(variegated)	Variegated Japanese Umbrella Pine
Solanum jasminoides	Potato Vine
Sophora japonica pendula	Japan Weeping Sophora, Weeping Scholar Tree
*Sorbus aucuparia**	Mountain Ash
Spiraea albiflora	Japanese White Spiraea
Spiraea billiardii X	Billiard Spiraea
Spiraea X bumalda	
'anthony waterer'	Anthony Waterer Spirea
Spiraea japonica ovalifolia	Mikado Spiraea
Spiraea prunifolia	Bridal Wreath
*Spiraea salicifolia**	Willowleaf Spiraea
*Spiraea tomentosa**	Hardhack Spiraea, Steeplebush
Spiraea thunbergii	Thunberg Spirea
Spiraea X vanhouttei	Vanhoutte Spirea
Stewartia pseudo-camellia	Japanese Stewartia - not used until after 1874.
Styrax japonica	Japanese Snowbell
*Symphoricarpus albus laevigatus**	Snowberry, Waxberry
*Symphoricarpus orbiculatus**	Indian Currant, Coral-berry
Syringa amurensis japonica	Japanese Tree Lilac - not used until after 1876.
Syringa chinensis	Chinese Lilac
*Syringa persica**	Persian Lilac

Syringa villosa	Late Lilac - not used until after 1882.
Syringa vulgaris var. alphonse	Double Bluish Lilac, Lavalle Lilac
Tamarix gallica var. indica	French Tamarisk
Tamarix pentandra	Five-stamen Tamarisk - not used until after 1883.
Taxus baccata var. aurea	Golden Yew
Taxus baccata var. elegantissima	Silver Tinted Variety
Taxus baccata var. stricta	Irish Yew
Taxus cuspidata	Japanese Yew
Taxus cuspidata 'nana'	Dwarf Japanese Yew
Thuja orientalis either var. elegantissima or aurea	Chinese Golden Arbor Vitae
Tilia americana *	American Linden
Tilia tomentosa	White or Silver-leaved Linden
Tsuga canadensis var. 'fremd'	
Tsuga canadensis var. globosa	
Tsuga canadensis var. macrophylla	
Tsuga canadensis pendula	Sargent Weeping Hemlock
Tsuga sieboldii	Southern Japanese or Siebold Hemlock
Ulmus americana *	American Elm
Ulmus glabra camperdownii	Camperdown Elm
Ulmus parvifolia *	Chinese Elm
Ulmus pumila *	Siberian Elm
Ulmus sp. *	Elms - "majestic at all seasons"
Viburnum lantana	Wayfaring Tree
Viburnum opulus	European Cranberry Bush
Viburnum opulus var. roseum *	Guelder Rose
Viburnum tomentosum var. sterlile *	Japanese Snowball
Weigela florida	Rosy Weigela - "They form one of our staple plants for the construction of any group of shrubs". Parsons
Weigela florida var. variegata	Variegated-leaved Weigelia
Weigela florida variegata (dwarf form)	Variegated Dwarf Weigelia
Wisteria floribunda	Japanese Wisteria
Wisteria frutescens *	American Wisteria
Wisteria sinensis var. alba & purpurea *	Chinese Wisteria
Xanthoceras sorbifolia	Chinese Flowering Chestnut - "rare and beautiful shrub"
Yucca filamentosa *	Adam's Needle, Yucca
Yucca recurvifolia	Yucca
Zelkova serrata	Graybark Elm

FIGURE CREDITS

Figure 1 - From Thomas Hill's, THE GARDENERS LABYRINTH (1577).

Figures 2, 3, 4, 5, 7, 9, 42, 43 - Drawn by the authors.

Figures 6, 13, 30, 32, 45 - Drawn by E. Emily Favretti.

Figure 8 - From Grace D. Wheeler's HOMES OF OUR ANCESTORS IN STONINGTON (1903).

Figures 10, 11, 28, 34, 35 - Photographs by the authors.

Figure 12 - "Mansion House With Figures" - Collection of the John Warren House, Brookline, Massachusetts. Photo courtesy of the Metropolitan Museum of Art.

Figure 14 - "View of the Seat of Colonel Boyd, Portsmouth, New Hampshire" - By permission of the Trustees of the Phillips Exeter Academy, Exeter, New Hampshire.

Figure 15 - Photo courtesy of Colonial Williamsburg, Incorporated.

Figure 16 - The Von Glummer reproduction of the original Vaughan Plan of Mount Vernon. Courtesy of the Mount Vernon Ladies Association, Mount Vernon, Virginia.

Figure 17 - Garden plans drawn by Samuel McIntire for the Elias Hasket Derby Mansion, Salem, Massachusetts. Photo courtesy of the Essex Institute, Salem, Massachusetts.

Figures 18, 21, 23, 24, 25, 26, 40 - From Andrew Jackson Downing's A TREATISE ON THE THEORY AND PRACTICE OF LANDSCAPE GARDENING (1849).

Figures 19, 20, 22, 39 - From Andrew Jackson Downing's COTTAGE RESIDENCES (1856).

Figures 29, 33 - From Jacob Weidenmann's BEAUTIFYING COUNTRY HOMES (1870).

Figures 26, 27, 31, 36, 41 - From Charles Henderson's PICTURESQUE GARDENING (1901).

Figure 37 - Knox Foundation, Hartford, Connecticut.

Figure 38 - From *Living Bicentennial Floral Designs,* Cooperative Extension Service, South Dakota State University.

Figure 44 - Photo by T.C. Sandson.

INDEX

"alleys" 17

animals, 25, 31, 36, 45

apple, Porter, 8

arabesque, 47, 48, 72

arbor, 18, 22, 25, 34, 35

architecture, Gothic, 30, 42, 43, 55; Greek revival, 41; Italianate, 41, 42, 43, 61; Tudor, 42

Barber, John Warner, 9

bees, 18, 22

belt road, 30

Bray, Mary Mathews, 11

Bridgeman, Charles, 32

Brown, Lancelot ("Capability") 32-33

carpet bedding, 69, 70, 72

cascade, 51

cast iron, 55, 60, 61, 64, 66, 74, 75, 77-78

central axial vista, 15, 27, 61

city lot gardens, 36

curbing, 11, 18, 22

Davis, Andrew Jackson, 43

dooryard, 11, 19, 20, 22, 23, 77

Downing, Andrew Jackson, 41-57, 64, 67, 69

drives, 41, 43, 44, 45, 54, 57, 77, 79. See also belt road.

Elias Hasket Derby House, 40

enclosed gardens, 15, 21, 22, 25, 26, 28, 29, 33, 35, 36, 37

English gardens, 15, 18, 20, 21, 27, 29, 30; Claremont, Stowe, 32; "English landscape", 31, 37; influence of, 37, 38, 41

farmstead, 19-22

faults, reproduction, 10-13

fences, 11, 23, 26, 35, 61, 64, 65, 74, 77-78; height of, 35-36; palings & pickets, 11, 21; picket, 21, 36, 64; rail, 16, 18; rustic, 33; solid board, 36; wattle, 15

flower beds, 12, 28, 34, 36, 37, 38, 44, 45, 47, 54, 57, 72, 77. See also arabesque, parterre, knot garden, carpet bedding, rosarium.

flowers, ancient gardens, & parterres, 18, 29; in American central axis garden, 34, 35; annuals, 23, 47; banished, 30, 32; craftsmen's & workmen's, 77-79; Downing, 41, 44, 45, 47,

About the Authors

Rudy J. Favretti is Professor of Landscape Architecture at the University of Connecticut in Storrs. He is an authority in landscape history and has advised on the restoration and reproduction of many important gardens. Joy Favretti, his wife, is a botanist and a graduate of Cornell University.

The Favrettis not only work together in writing about gardens but they also care for extensive vegetable and flower gardens at their home in Mansfield. They are the parents of three children.